THIS BOOK IS DEDICATED TO...

MRS. ANNE KENNEDY

The "First-Lady" of Evangelism Explosion International. Anne, along with her husband Jim, founded the ministry back in 1962. Anne has faithfully served as a trainer in the ministry leading many thousands to Christ, and encouraging the work worldwide.

MRS. ANN SORENSEN

All of those who are married in the ministry of Evangelism Explosion serve together as couples. Ann is my best friend and fellow laborer in the Gospel of Jesus Christ. God has gifted me with her, and made the journey sweet beyond words. Ann is a great encouragement to the workers worldwide as we travel and train others to be witnesses for Jesus Christ.

Evangelism Explosion's two Ann(e)s, pictured together at the opening of our new location for the D. James Kennedy Center for Christian Statesmanship in Washington, D.C. Summer 2013.

YOUR STORY COUNTS

SHARING THE MOST IMPORTANT STORY OF YOUR LIFE

DR. JOHN B. SORENSEN

GREEN TREE PRESS
FORT LAUDERDALE, FL

Published in Fort Lauderdale, Florida by Green Tree Press.

Edited by John Aman, Debbie Revitzer, Mike Ferraguti, and Hannah Sorensen. Cover design by Cheryl Philips.

ISBN: 978-0-9828721-6-1

TABLE OF CONTENTS

INTRODUCTION

Your story counts.

It may seem obvious, but I am amazed at how many Christians do not think their story counts for much of anything. Perhaps they intellectually agree that their testimony has value, but they still imagine their story to be a bit lackluster. "My story is no big deal," they say. It's possible that they came to Christ as a child and don't have a clearcut moment that they can point to where their lives changed. Certainly they don't have one of those superstar testimonies that grips you and puts you on the edge of your seat. "Boring," one might say of his or her supposedly ho-hum story. "I just don't see how mine could count for much."

The conversation does beg a few questions like, "What is a story?" and, "Where might it count?"

Others understand that they do have a story, and share it occasionally, but do not see how God can use it. "How do you start?" they ask. "Wouldn't it be weird to just throw it into a conversation?"

On top of these questions, we should ask what the Bible says about our story and the expectations Christ has for how we use it in our daily lives. Can He really use your story to affect others and assist people in putting their trust in Him?

This books aims to answer these questions and help you prepare a testimony, or many testimonies, that you can share as a regular part of your life. You'll find illustrations of others' stories and see how they are used. Our goal is to help you find an actual way to get into and use the story that God has given you. After all, what good is a story if you don't know what to say, or when and where to share it? The goal is to help prepare you to be able to *"Always be ready to tell everyone who asks you why you believe as you do"* (1 Peter 3:15 NLT). In this way, we become His witnesses.

I've met people who are natural born witnesses. Dr. Bill Bright fits that description. He would get on an elevator and say, "Up down, up down, one day we'll go up and never come down!" Then he would start a conversation with others on the elevator about the confidence God has given him. It would often lead to his being able to share Christ!

As an aside, I tried that one day. I boarded a packed elevator with a family of people dressed to go to a party. I looked at one of the children, smiled, and said, "Up down, up down, one day we'll go up and never come down!" To my amazement, the father asked how I could have such confidence. They actually got off the elevator on my floor and let me share Christ with them. Amazing!

While I've not met him, there is a story about a Mr. Jenner that blesses my heart and shows the value of intentional witnessing. It comes from Dr. Francis Dixon, a Baptist pastor in England during the early 20th century. He was well known for his revival ministry in New Zealand and Australia.

One Sunday evening Dr. Dixon asked a man to give his personal testimony of salvation. The man spoke out:

I was in the Royal Navy stationed in Sydney, Australia. One night I was walking down George Street when suddenly out popped this old gray-haired man who said: "Excuse me sir, could I ask you a question? I hope you won't be offended. But if you were to die tonight, do you know where you would spend eternity? The Bible says it will be either in Hell or in Heaven. Would you kindly think about that please? Thank you! And God Bless you. Toodely doo!" And he left.

I had never been asked that question before, and I couldn't get it out of my mind. When I got back to England I sought out a pastor and was converted to Christ.

Seven weeks later there was a Gospel campaign at Dr. Dixon's church. He asked one of the Evangelistic team members to share how he got saved:

A number of years ago I was in the Royal Navy stationed in Sydney Australia. One night on George Street a little old gray-haired man stopped me and said, "Excuse me sir, could I ask you a question? I hope you won't be offended. But if you were to die tonight, do you know where you would spend eternity? The Bible says it will be either in Hell or in Heaven. Would you kindly think about that please? Thank you! And God Bless you. Toodely doo!" And he left. I went back to England and sought out a Christian businessman and accepted Christ as my Savior and Lord."

Several months later Dr. Dixon was in Perth, Australia, conducting a Gospel meeting. He said, "I have to share something with you all," and he told them about what had happened in these two men's lives.

A man in the audience began waving his arms. "What is it?" asked Dr. Dixon. "I'm another! I was in Sydney... George Street... Toodely doo! I accepted Christ!"

Dr. Dixon came home to his church in England and shared these stories with his congregation. A woman stood up and said, "Dr. Dixon, I'm another! Sydney... Toodely doo! Trusted Christ."

Later Dixon was at the Keswick Pastor's Conference and shared these stories. A pastor stood up... "I'm another!... Sydney... Toodely doo!... Trusted Christ."

One year later Dr. Dixon was at a missions conference in India and shared these accounts and a missionary stood up: "I'm another! Sydney... Toodely doo!... Converted."

Months later Dr. Dixon was at a Christian Businessman's Convention in Jamaica and he shared these accounts. A businessman stood up... "I'm another! Toodely doo!"

Where do you think Dr. Dixon went next? He traveled to Sydney, Australia before going back to England and spoke to a Christian businessman. He told him the story and asked, "Do you know this old man?"

"Oh sure," was the reply. "Everyone has heard of Mr. Jenner. He's been doing this for over twenty years. He's very feeble now since he just came out of the hospital, and he's almost blind."

Dr. Dixon asked, "Would you take me to him?"

"Of course," the businessman said.

Dr. Dixon introduced himself and began to tell the story of one conversion after another. The little old gray-haired man began to weep uncontrollably.

Dr. Dixon was concerned and said, "Excuse me sir. What's the matter?"

The little old gray-haired man said, "This is the first time in 23 years that I have ever known of someone coming to Christ through my testimony!"

People like Dr. Bright, and Mr. Jenner, are fantastic to be around. They always seem to find a way to get into a spiritual conversation.

But the truth is that most of us are not like that. We are much more shy about starting conversations with a spiritual purpose. If that is you, then there is good news.

The ministry of Evangelism Explosion was founded by Dr. D. James Kennedy. Dr. Kennedy would often remind me, and others, how he had been a "card-carrying member" of Cowards Anonymous®. (There actually isn't such a group, but maybe there should be?) He said that he had a yellow stripe that ran up his back and somehow attached firmly to his jaw. Whenever an opportunity came up, this infirmity would take over, preventing him from speaking. I had no such knowledge of Dr. Kennedy.

He was a bold and consistent witness for Christ in his everyday life. What changed?

He would tell you that the difference was his being trained. Once he knew what he was going to say, the fear went away, "like the dew before a rising sun." Jim Kennedy learned from a man named Kennedy Smartt, who had learned from a man named Bill Iverson…and thus the story goes on.

The point is that learning to share your story, and then Christ's story, is something that one can learn and excel at. I find that to be very heartening.

How wonderful it will be to hear someone in Heaven say, "God really used you to lead me to Christ. What He did in your life made a real difference to me! Thank you for sharing!"

May it be.

Soli Deo Gloria.

BRYAN'S STORY

B efore I received eternal life, as a young teenager, I was searching for life. I tried different avenues to gain that satisfaction. I played rugby for the village team and enjoyed the camaraderie, but there was something missing. So I moved on to something else, searching for life.

I was doing an engineering apprenticeship at age 17 when my best friend came into work and said, "Bryan, I got saved last night." I didn't have a clue what he meant. I asked, "What do you mean, John?"

"Well," John said, "I gave my life to Jesus."

I didn't know what to think. John was the kind of guy who would collect antiques, and then he would move on to something else. So I thought, this is his "Christian bit" and he's going to move on shortly. But rather than it waning, he became stronger and more enthusiastic. After about eight months, I asked him, "Can I come along to church with you?"

I was just over 17 when I went to church for the first time. For about six months I listened to the Gospel being preached, but I just resolved that I would better my life on my own. I'll stop doing this, I'll stop doing that; but I found that the more I tried, the worse I got.

One evening, a dear friend preached from Hebrews 13:13, *"Let us go therefore to him without the camp, bearing his reproach."* He shared about Jesus dying on the cross, abandoned and alone. God spoke to me that night, September 6, 1959, and I gave my life to Christ.

I immediately felt a lightness. How it came to me, I don't know. But I left that building and I quoted a verse of a hymn:

> *Heaven above is softer blue*
> *Earth around is sweeter green;*
> *Something lives in every hue*
> *Christless eyes have never seen*
> *Birds with gladder songs o'erflow*
> *Flowers with deeper beauties shine.*
>
> George Wade Robinson
> Loved with Everlasting Love, Baptist Hymn Book
> (Psalms and & Hymns Trust, London, 1962)

And it's been like that for me.

I used to use bad language quite a lot. It was every other word. But to my amazement when I went in to work the next day, I wasn't swearing! Many of my co-workers said, "Your speech is different. Why?"

I said, "Well, last night, I gave my life to Christ."

I found Him who said, "I have come that they may have life, and that they may have it more abundantly" (John 10:10 NKJV). He brings purpose and joy, satisfaction and hope, something I never had before.

God so changed my life that I entered the ministry in 1974, learned about Evangelism Explosion (EE) in 1980, and have continued ever since in pastoral and EE ministry.

Praise the Lord!

ONE

WHAT'S YOUR STORY?

YOU CAN'T SHARE YOUR STORY
IF YOU DON'T HAVE A STORY

"But this is the new covenant I will make with the people of Israel on that day," says the LORD. "I will put my instructions deep within them, and I will write them on their hearts. I will be their God, and they will be my people."

Jeremiah 31:33 NLT

E vangelism Explosion International is a ministry that began back in 1962 under the direction and leadership of Dr. D. James Kennedy, the senior pastor of Coral Ridge Presbyterian Church in Fort Lauderdale, Florida. Since its founding, the ministry has grown to literally cover the world, becoming the first Christian ministry to be active in every nation on earth back in 1996. During our 50-plus year history, we have, by

5

God's grace, trained millions of Christians to be witnesses for Jesus Christ all over the world.

I say we, because I've been a part of the ministry since the early 1990s, when I came to know the Lord through the ministry. It was also through the ministry of Evangelism Explosion that I first learned how to witness. Somewhere in the middle of all that, and by God's grace, my wife, Ann and I became part of the ministry. We joined the staff in the first part of 1997.

LEADERSHIP TRAINING CLINICS

One of the core activities of the ministry is conducting Leadership Training Clinics where we equip and train leaders within the local church to be able to witness, and to train others in their congregations to witness as well. In 2013, we conducted over 2,000 clinics worldwide.

I had the privilege of attending a clinic taught by Dr. D. James Kennedy back in 1995. It was an awesome week of encouragement and vision. Each morning we spent time in a small prayer group, and we used those prayer groups as we worked on particular assignments—like the assignment where we developed a personal testimony.

While we were working on our testimonies, there was one particular member of the team that could not develop one for his life! No matter what we tried he just got more and more frustrated. Then, all of a sudden, it came to him. I remember him grabbing the table and blurting out, "I need to get saved!" Amazing really. But all the more amazing when you realize this man was a mainline church pastor. In fact, he had been a pastor for over 40 years!

We took him at his word, gathered together, joined hands, and prayed with him that Jesus would become the Lord and Savior of his life. Tears were streaming down his face as he got up to tell the entire class what had just happened. Almost in shock, we sat back down to continue the work of developing our testimonies. All of a sudden the words just flowed from him, and his testimony came immediately.

It dawned on me then how very important a personal relationship with Jesus Christ is to being able to develop a testimony. In fact, without one, a real testimony is simply not possible.

By the way, my pastor friend went back to his church on Sunday morning and told his congregation what happened. He said, "For many years I have preached about a Jesus that I knew about. Today I preach to you a Jesus whom I know!" As I understood it, a number of people got saved that Sunday!

Since that day, I've come to understand that the action of this particular pastor is not that unusual. The truth is that during our clinics worldwide quite a number of pastors give their hearts to Christ each and every year. There have been clinics in the Third World where the number has been as high as 70%!

One of the reasons, they tell us, is that the ministry possesses the clearest Gospel presentation that they have ever heard. But on top of that is the fact that we work on a personal testimony, and you can't share a testimony if you don't have a testimony. And a real testimony of transformation only comes by being transformed and possessing the Power of the Holy Spirit to live beyond yourself.

That does lead to another question, doesn't it? How do you receive the Power of the Holy Spirit? Well, we know the answer--believe in the Lord Jesus Christ and accept Him as your personal Lord and Savior. Ultimately that is done through the hearing and believing of the Gospel of Jesus Christ. This is what the Bible refers to as being born again.

WHAT IS THE GOSPEL?

So what is the Gospel? Well, before I answer that, allow me to ask you two questions. They will help to clarify what it is that you believe. Please take a moment and write down your answers in the white space next to the question.

Diagnostic Question #1

Are you absolutely certain that if you died today you would go to Heaven? Circle One: Yes / No / Hope So

Diagnostic Question #2

Suppose you were to die today and stand before God, and He were to ask you, "Why should I let you into My Heaven?" What would you say? Write your answer here:

_____

_____

_____

_____

Please don't continue until you have answered these two questions. Obviously, I can't read your answers. But they are important for you as we talk about what the Bible says.

With regard to the first question, one of the reasons the Bible exists is so that we can know, for certain, that we will go to Heaven when we die. In the Bible we read, *"I have written this to you who believe in the name of the Son of God, so that you may know you have eternal life"* (1 John 5:13 NLT).

And with regard to the second question, there is only one way to answer it, according to the Bible.

GRACE

Heaven, eternal life, living forever in God's presence, is a free gift. As a gift, it is not earned or deserved. Also, it is not something that can be paid for or purchased. Consider what the Bible says:

> *For the wages of sin is death, but the free gift of God is eternal life through Christ Jesus our Lord.*
>
> Romans 3:23 NLT

> *For it is by grace you have been saved, through faith— and this is not from yourselves, it is the gift of God— not by works, so that no one can boast.*
>
> Ephesians 2:8-9 NIV

Like any real gift, Heaven must be received freely. Sometimes we will intellectually agree with a statement like this, but actively do all we can to disagree. What I mean is that we say we accept the gift, but then we do everything we can to pay God back for what He has so graciously offered to us.

Look again at your answer to the second question. The most common answer that we receive worldwide to the second question has to do with actions or activities that a person will do in order to make themselves acceptable before God. In this way, we think we can "earn" Heaven.

It's a bit like the jobs that we do. After we have worked for a week or two, we don't go into our boss and say, "Will you please give the gift of a paycheck?" That would be ridiculous. We say, "Please pay me what I've earned." Or, if we're a bit more forward we might shout, "Give me my money!" We've earned it. It's ours. But not so with regards to Heaven.

It can never be.

The bottom line is that we couldn't pay for it even if we wanted to because of a very real problem that we have called sin.

MAN

We are all sinners. Therefore, it is simply not possible for us to save ourselves.

We really don't like to use the word "sin" these days, but like it or not, sin is a real problem because sin separates us from an All-Holy and Perfect God.

What is sin? Normally, when I ask people to define sin, I hear things like murder, robbery and adultery. But sin is much more than the "big things." And sin is not limited to actions. Sin can be an attitude, a thought, a word. Perhaps worst of all, sin can be not doing something that we should have done.

Here is a good one sentence definition of sin: Anything that falls short of God's perfect standard.

For everyone has sinned; we all fall short of God's glorious standard.

Romans 3:23 NLT

As Bob Thune, our pastor in Omaha, used to say, "All means all, that's all all means!"

I think most of us agree that we are not perfect. But we don't know that we are in truly bad shape.

Let me illustrate that our sin is far more serious than we realize or even want to admit. With the thousands of thoughts, thousands of words and thousands of actions that take place in a single day in each of our lives, I wonder how many times we fall short of God's perfect standard. One hundred…fifty… twenty-five?

For our illustration, we will be exceptionally good people and only have three sins on our list. In reality, the number is much higher. Yet, even at our three sins a day, in a year's time that adds up to well over a thousand. With the average age now well into the seventies, even with this conservative estimate, we will amass a record of more than 70,000 times that we fell short of God's perfect standard. Can you imagine walking into a traffic court with 70,000 speeding tickets and declaring to the judge that you are a really good driver? Ludicrous!

We are not pretty good people, we are serious sinners. As mentioned earlier, the wages of sin is death. People often state that they only want God to be fair. To be fair is to give what is deserved.

You and I are sinners. So, if God was fair and simply gave us the wages we have earned, we would be dead. In fact, that is what we are as sinners—spiritually dead.

On top of this, as we've already talked about, God does have a standard. He told us that if we want to get into Heaven based on our own activities, we merely need to be, *"perfect, even as your Father in Heaven is perfect"* (Matthew 5:48 NLT).

We are far from that. Hopefully you can see how no amount of good works, regardless how good, can save anyone.

As you reflect on your answer to question number two, what were you trusting in? Who did you refer to in your answer? If it was you, and the good things that you do, I hope you can see how that answer can not work. So then, if you cannot save yourself, how can you be saved?

God must have an entirely different way.

GOD

God is merciful and does not want to punish us. But God is also just and must punish sin. Two short verses validate these vitally important dimensions of God's character.

God is love.

1 John 4:8b NLT

I (God) do not excuse the guilty.

Exodus 34:7 NLT

So, on one hand God loves us very much, but the same Bible that tells us of His great love also tells us that He is just and must punish our sins.

So it would seem that we have a problem, a serious problem. It is a problem we cannot solve for ourselves. The Good News is that God solved our problem in the person of Jesus Christ!

JESUS CHRIST

Here is where the Person and Work of Jesus Christ are essential. Jesus is God, born into this world as a man. This is called the incarnation and is celebrated each Christmas. The first verses of John's Gospel emphasize this truth:

In the beginning was the Word, and the Word was with God, and the Word was God.... And the Word became flesh and dwelt among us, and we beheld His glory, the

14

glory as of the only begotten of the Father, full of grace and truth.

John 1:1,14 NKJV

You will notice that "Word" is capitalized. This is because it is a name, or a title, for Jesus. So, this verse could be read: In the beginning was Jesus, and Jesus was with God, and Jesus was God.... And Jesus became flesh and dwelt among us, and we beheld His glory, the glory as of the only begotten of the Father, full of grace and truth.

While Jesus accomplished so much in His brief time on this earth, there is one accomplishment that stands head and shoulders above all the rest. Jesus died on the cross to pay the penalty for our sins and rose again from the dead to prove He had purchased a place in Heaven for us.

The last sentence Jesus spoke from the cross before breathing His last breath was, *"It is finished!"* Actually, in the language He used, it is a single word: Tetelestai, which is translated "paid in full." Having lived a sinless life, He paid the sin debt of every person who trusts in Him for forgiveness.

All of us, like sheep, have strayed away. We have left God's paths to follow our own. Yet the Lord laid on him [Jesus] the sins of us all.

Isaiah 53:6 NLT

For God made Christ, who never sinned, to be the offering for our sin, so that we could be made right with God through Christ.

2 Corinthians 5:21 NLT

Having perfectly satisfied the righteous requirements of God's holy law, Jesus died as our substitute, in our place. This is the ultimate expression of the holy love and holy justice of God.

But God showed his great love for us by sending Christ to die for us while we were still sinners. And since we have been made right in God's sight by the blood of Christ, he will certainly save us from God's condemnation.

Romans 5:8-9 NLT

The wages for sin now having been paid, we can become the recipients of the gift of eternal life. This gift can only be received one way—by faith.

FAITH

Faith is the key to Heaven's door. But it is so widely misunderstood today because we use the word in so many ways.

Many times, when people say "faith," they mean an agreement to a group of facts. For them, it's an acknowledgement to a truth that they hold. But this is not the kind of faith that will save anyone, because saving faith is not simply head knowledge.

I have faith that there was a man named George Washington, who was the first President of the United States. I've never met George, nor have I ever met anyone who has met him. Yet I still believe he existed and did, for the most part, what people say that he did. But I have no relationship with George Washington. I do not expect him to show up and do anything for me today. For most of my life, that is the kind of "faith" I had in Jesus. And that kind of faith will not save anyone. Knowing about someone and knowing someone are very different matters.

Another type of faith that people mistake for saving faith is temporary faith. When a loved one gets sick, we might pray for him or her. That is health faith. When we fly in an airplane to go on vacation, we might pray for safety. That is traveling faith. These are temporary matters; when the loved one is no longer sick or the trip is over, we don't need that faith any longer. Temporary faith will not save anyone.

So, what is saving faith? Saving faith is trusting in Jesus Christ alone for your salvation. It is trusting what He did on the cross to pay for your sins. When you trust Christ, you stop trusting in your own supposed goodness, or religiosity, or any long list of good deeds.

The apostle Paul is the most famous missionary in the history of the Christian church. While imprisoned in the city of Philippi, he had a dramatic encounter with the Roman jailer who was working the third shift. You can read the account in Acts 16:25-40. Shortly after midnight and following a great earthquake, the jailer posed a profound question to Paul, who responded with an even more profound answer.

> *Then he* [the jailer] *called for a light, ran in, and fell down trembling before Paul and Silas. And he brought them out and said, "Sirs, what must I do to be saved?" So they said, "Believe on the Lord Jesus Christ, and you will be saved...."* (Acts 16:31 NLT)

Remember, your only contribution to your salvation is your sin. It is your sin, which separates you from God, that makes your salvation through the work of Christ necessary.

A helpful illustration will give you a visual as to how this must apply to you and your life. In your mind I want you to see the two of us sitting in chairs around your kitchen table. At the side of the table next to me is an empty kitchen chair. To illustrate saving faith, I will pose three questions regarding that empty chair. First, do you believe that chair exists? Is it real? The obvious answer is yes. Next, do you believe that the empty chair would hold me if I sat in it? Again you would answer in the affirmative.

Finally, why isn't that empty chair holding me up right now? Because I am not sitting in that empty chair.

Now, we are going to label our three chairs. The chair in which you are sitting has a label bearing your name. The chair on which I am sitting is labeled the "John" chair. The empty chair is labeled the "Jesus" chair.

All of us are born sitting in the chair bearing our name. Sinners though we are, we come to the conclusion that God should let us into Heaven because we are basically good people, trying our best, not intentionally harming anyone. We are sitting on the chair of our good works.

So, if we had to provide an answer as to why God should let us into Heaven, we would respond, "I should get in because I am a good person, trying my best and not intentionally harming anyone."

If you or I answered that way, we would enter a Christ-less eternity in hell. This is exactly what we deserve.

To receive the gift of eternal life, we must get up from the chair bearing our name and sit down in the Jesus chair. We transfer our trust from ourselves to Jesus Christ alone for our salvation.

The question to you at this point is simple and straightforward. Are you sitting in the chair bearing your name? If you are, it is time for you to confess your sin, acknowledge that you deserve to go to hell, thank God for sending Christ to die on the cross for your sin and receive Christ as your Savior and Lord.

But to all who believed him and accepted him, he gave the right to become children of God. They are reborn—not with a physical birth resulting from human passion or plan, but a birth that comes from God.

John 1:12 NLT

Christ as Savior calls you to agree that you are a sinner and Christ is the only Savior.

Christ as Lord calls you to repent (which means to make a behavioral U-turn), agreeing that your way is the wrong way and that Christ's way is the right way. It means that you get down off of the throne in your heart and let Jesus take His rightful place on that throne.

DECISION POINT

Does this make sense to you? Because this is such an important matter let's clarify just what it involves. It means that you need to:

- Transfer your trust from what you have been doing to what Christ has done for you on His cross.

- Accept the living Christ as Savior. Jesus is alive today and says, *"Look! I stand at the door and knock. If you hear my voice and open the door, I will come in..."* (Revelation 3:20 NLT)

- Receive Jesus Christ as your Lord. Give Him the "driver's seat" and "controls" of your life, not the "back seat."

- Repent. Be willing to turn from anything that is not pleasing to Him. He will reveal His will to you as you grow in your relationship with Him.

Now, if this is what you really want, you can go to God in prayer right where you are. You can receive His gift of eternal life through Jesus Christ right now.

For it is by believing in your heart that you are made right with God, and it is by confessing with your mouth that you are saved... For "Everyone who calls on the name of the Lord will be saved."

Romans 10:10,13 NLT

If you want to receive the gift of eternal life through Jesus Christ, then call on Him asking Him for this gift right now. Here's a suggested prayer:

"Lord Jesus, thank You for Your gift of eternal life. I know I'm a sinner and do not deserve eternal life. But You loved me so You died and rose from the grave to purchase a place in Heaven for me. I now trust in You alone for eternal life and repent of my sin. Please take control as Lord of my life. Thank you so much!"

If this prayer is the sincere desire of your heart, look at what Jesus promises to those who believe in Him: *"Most assuredly, I say to you, he who believes in Me has everlasting life"* (John 6:47 NKJV).

Welcome to the family of God!

Once we have received the great gift of eternal life, the Bible tells us that we are filled with God's Holy Spirit and are given the ability to live with a power beyond our own. This infilling of the Holy Spirit begins to write a story on our hearts of God's interactions and faithfulness in our lives. And this is the story that we will examine in this book. This is the greatest story of your life.

OLGA'S STORY

KAZAKHSTAN

K azakhstan was part of the Soviet Union for seventy years. During communism, nobody talked about God. After the collapse of the Soviet Union in 1991, Kazakhstan opened the doors for missionaries from South Korea and America to come.

Growing up as a teenager, I always wondered if there was a God. I asked my parents, but they could tell me nothing.

In college, I studied to be a Russian and English translator. Afterwards, I searched for an internship. I went to a village where Americans were coming to do summer English camp for children, and they were looking for translators. They accepted me for the six-week internship.

It was the first time I ever met Americans. They were so friendly—smiling, caring and loving. They had some inner joy and peace that I never had but wanted so much. I remember growing up always being worried about everything: what kind of job I will have after I graduate from college, who I will marry, etc. So, I asked one of the Americans why they are always so happy and joyful? The answer was, "We have not been like that always. It is Jesus who changed us." I was so amazed and excited that I finally met people who know God.

The next summer they came back to do the same summer camp at the same village. So, I had my second internship with them. This time my friend asked me if he could pray with me. That day I received eternal life. The next day I woke up with the feeling of lightness, ready to fly like a bird. I could not understand why I felt so different, but it was like my heavy burden and worries had suddenly disappeared. It was a good thing because it made me able to face the next part of my journey.

In 2009, I was diagnosed with cancer at just 28 years of age. I could not believe it happened to me. When somebody in Kazakhstan gets such diagnosis, they are not expected to live long. My family and friends began preparing to lose me soon, but God had another plan. He sent His "angels" to pray for me, faithful brothers and sisters in Christ who believed that God can bring a miraculous healing. Some of them went beyond and offered to bring me to America. They took me to the hospital and when the doctors saw how serious my case was, I was not given much hope. I had one of the most rare types of cancer called Adeno-Cystic Carcinoma, located in the sinus area near the eye orbit, and it was the last stage.

I had surgery but the doctor could remove only a small part of the tumor through the nose. Complete removal of the tumor was not an option due to the location and the size of the tumor

(5.2 cm x 2.4 cm x 2.3 cm). The doctor said if he tried to remove the tumor completely, I would die in the middle of that surgery. Radiation therapy was my only option but I could not have the standard radiation due to the close location of the tumor to the brain stem. There were only five clinics in the U.S. that provided proton-beam radiation therapy that I needed. Radiation therapy lasted for two months. I tolerated it very poorly from the very beginning. I had nausea all the time. I could not eat because my mouth area was burned by radiation. My face was red as a tomato. It was the most difficult time in my life but, again, with constant support of my friends, God gave me strength to endure it.

After the treatment was over, I went back to Kazakhstan. A few months after the treatment, my MRI images showed no evidence of a residual tumor. My doctor was amazed because, normally, he said the tumor shrinks, but in my case it was completely gone. Science cannot explain it, and it is still a mystery to me how Jesus removed it completely. Praise the Lord! There is truly nothing impossible for our God.

I believe God has healed me. I have no more headaches, my energy is back and I feel more healthy than I've ever been. What the enemy meant for evil, God turned into good. Many of my friends and family got encouraged by witnessing what God has done in my life. It has been four years, and I'm still cancer free, praising the Lord for every day of my life.

I used to be a big planner, setting goals and planning my life years ahead, basically living in the future and not in the present. What I learned from this is to live one day at a time and not to take life for granted. God said in His word, *"How do you know what your life will be like tomorrow?"* (James 4:14 NLT).

I don't know why God has allowed this to happen, but I know that He has changed my whole life. It has grown my faith, and I know that there is nothing impossible for our BIG God. Life is relatively short on this earth, and only God knows how much longer we have left to live. How will I use this time? I don't want to waste it. I choose to live every day of my life bringing glory to Him, sharing what He has done, and fulfilling the purpose He's chosen me for. This is the only thing that will last and has true value.

Last year, God opened the door for me to go to Bible school. I have learned to love the Word of God, to love my neighbor, and to start each day with quiet time with Him. I committed my life to full-time Christian service because there is nothing that brings me more joy than to share about His love and His mighty power to do the impossible. He is the God of miracles. We should never doubt His power, but believe.

TWO

YOUR STORY COUNTS

YOUR TESTIMONY MATTERS FOR THE KINGDOM OF GOD

Then I heard a loud voice shouting across the heavens, "It has come at last—salvation and power and the Kingdom of our God, and the authority of his Christ. For the accuser of our brothers and sisters has been thrown down to earth—the one who accuses them before our God day and night. And they have defeated him by the blood of the Lamb and by their testimony. And they did not love their lives so much that they were afraid to die."

Revelation 12:10-11 NLT

What do you think of when you hear the word "testimony"? How would you define it? If you were to close your eyes and imagine what a "typical" testimony should sound like, what would you hear in your imagination?

What I find that people think of when they hear the word "testimony" is some super fantastic story of a miracle like one I could tell of my friend (I'll call Shakil) from Central Asia.

SHAKIL'S TESTIMONY

Shakil was trained as a field worker for Evangelism Explosion. After his training, he was going back to his home village for a wedding. This wedding that was to be conducted in the context of a very tribal form of Islam, so an imam would be responsible to perform the ceremony.

Two weeks before the wedding, according to tradition, the imam tied a chain around the waist of the bride-to-be and put a lock on it. During the wedding, when it came time for the groom and bride to be joined together, the imam would use the key, open the lock, and remove the chain. This would symbolize that the woman was free to be married to the man.

During this particular ceremony, it came time for the key; but the imam could not find the key anywhere. He had tons of keys, but none of the keys that he had would open the lock around the bride's waist.

The imam was having a fit because if he could not find the key then the couple would not be allowed to be wed. So he postponed the wedding by saying, "I'll find the key. Tomorrow we will finish the wedding."

So they all came back the next day for the continuation of the wedding, and he had many keys. He tried them all, but none of them would open the lock to free the bride from the chain. He was just about to proclaim that the couple could not be wed when Shakil bravely stood up in the back and said, "Wait, wait, wait! I know what the problem is! This is not supposed to be a Muslim wedding. This is supposed to be a Christian wedding! And I can prove it to you—if when I pray God opens the lock, will you believe me that this is supposed to be a Christian wedding?"

They all said, "Yes!" (I mean, what was there to lose for them, right?)

So Shakil put his hands up in the air and started to pray; and literally while he was praying, they all heard a small click—the lock opened up! The people in the town fell down to their knees because they were so afraid of the God who had done this. This miracle gave him the chance to share the Gospel of Jesus Christ with everyone in the village and many put their faith in Jesus.

Of course, this led a certain group of religious leaders to be very unhappy with Shakil. A few days later they caught him on the road outside the village. They took some large rocks and stoned him, leaving what they thought was his dead body on the side of the road. Ladies from the village came out to get his body to wash and bury him. But while they were washing him, he awakened! After a few weeks of recovery, he went about continuing to witness and telling people about Jesus.

Finally, the leaders caught him on the road again and told him that if he did not leave that they were going to cut him up with knives and that they were pretty convinced that no God was going to be able to put him back together again.

That's when we decided to move him to another Central Asian nation where he continues to witness and train today.

Wow. Fantastic really, isn't it?

Some people think that when you hear the word "testimony" that you are talking about a story like Shakil's. Stories that seem like they come directly from the book of Acts. They make us rejoice in the movement of God in the lives of His people. They give us hope that He will also move through us.

The downside of these fantastical stories is that people will hear them at church, and often the first thing they assume is that their story is nothing like that. And because of that, it must not count for the kingdom of God. They think, "I have got nothing that could even be in the same league as that story." And so they keep quiet.

YOUR STORY COUNTS

Perhaps I've just described you. If that's true, you're not alone. Many of us believe that our story is too simple to matter—but it does. Your story is actually the exact thing that God will use for the advancement of His Kingdom and the praise of His Holy Name!

As a trainer in EE, I have taken out teams of people thousands of times to share the Gospel with others. I have seen people's seemingly "ordinary" testimonies be used by God repeatedly to lead people to Christ around the world. What I find as we go out is that every Christian's testimony is amazing and powerful.

On one of my teams, there was a sweet, little, old lady who said to me, "John, I have nothing to say. My testimony isn't powerful." Yet that night, she got to share her "simple" testimony while we were sharing with a person we met down at the beach, and her testimony became the very thing that allowed the Gospel to be heard! As the person we were sharing with bowed her head and prayed to accept Jesus Christ as her Lord and Savior, I saw a confidence come into my sweet trainee. She never again thought her story to be too small.

31

This happens so many times. God truly uses the base things of the world to confound the wise. In fact, that is exactly what God's Word says, but we forget that.

I have talked to a number of Christians around the world—sometimes even important church leaders—and asked them about the impact of their story and if they use their story everyday. Most say to me that their story is too small to matter. To them, it seems insignificant.

But I have a hard time justifying that when I read in the Bible in Revelation 12:11 NLT, *"And they have defeated him by the blood of the Lamb and by their testimony..."*

POWER TO LIVE

Because of what the Bible says, I'm convinced that our testimony must be an incredibly valuable possession. It seems to me that we in the Church need to become better at recognizing the story of God in our lives, and then be able, equipped, and encouraged to share that story on a regular basis. My belief is that if we did, we would use our unique and valuable stories as a tool for finding a lot of people open to hear the Gospel of Jesus Christ.

Please be encouraged—your testimony does matter. It matters in the kingdom of God. It is an incredibly valuable weapon

mony is powerful because of what Christ has done in us—not because of anything we have done ourselves.

Regardless of what our story is, it is God who has orchestrated all things to bring glory to the Father, Son, and Holy Ghost; and He will use our story (IF we are willing to declare it for Him) in wonderful and glorious ways. But we must recognize that He is the Great Creator who weaves the Grand Story.

THE GREAT STORY WEAVER

Sometimes I imagine God has a great switchboard in Heaven where He is weaving all the stories of His people into one, beautiful, Grand Story (what theologians call a metanarrative). Now, I am not sure if God actually uses a switchboard; but I do know that there is a beautiful, Grand Story of God's that is playing out in time and space all over the world.

God started with the beginning of the world when He created all things. *"In the beginning God created the heavens and the earth"* (Genesis 1:1 NLT). In the same chapter where we learn about how God created mankind, we also see that God (in three Persons—the Trinity) was there from the very beginning of the story: *"Then God said, Let us make human beings in our image, to be like us... So God created human beings in his own image. In the image of God he created them; male and female he created them"* (Genesis 1:26a, 27 NLT).

But after God breathed life into our ancestors, Adam and Eve, His human creations were tempted by the enemy in the Garden of Eden; and they decided that they wanted to be god in their own lives. They ate of the tree God commanded them not to and were enslaved for the rest of their lives to sin. Sin has never left humankind since that fateful day and, because of it, we are all dead in our sin.

Because of His holiness, God cannot look upon sin. Because of His justice, God must punish sin. The bad news is that there is a standard to be able to be with God because of His holiness and justice, and it is for us to be perfect. The only problem is that none of us can be perfect because of our sin, and the Bible says, *"All have sinned..."* (Romans 3:23 NLT)

Finally, there is a pronouncement about what happens to those that sin, *"for the wages of sin is death..."* (Romans 6:23a). And not only physical death, which came into the world with sin, but also spiritual death—being removed from God in every way.

God could have left the story there and wiped out mankind with the flood, but He had mercy on us and did not leave the story unfinished. Because of His great love, He doesn't want to punish us, His children. Romans 6:23 goes on to share the good news, *"but the free gift of God is eternal life..."* God has graciously offered a way to get back to Him. A way which He spelled out throughout history for us to clearly see.

Throughout the Old Testament, the children of God had to sacrifice lambs for their sins so they might be pure in the sight of God, and God was faithful with them—even when they were not faithful to Him. He wove the story in the Old Testament to foreshadow Christ's coming, when God Himself would come to earth to be the ultimate sacrifice to cleanse God's children of their sins. In the New Testament, Christ did come and live the perfect life, and He died on the cross taking the sin of the world on His shoulders. He defeated death and sin by His resurrection on that glorious Easter, and now we can be cleansed of our sin: *"If you confess with your mouth that Jesus is Lord and believe in your heart that God raised him from the dead..."* (Romans 10:9 NLT). We can have the perfect robes of Jesus and when the Father looks at us, He sees Christ's righteousness.

THE STORY GOES ON

After Christ's coming, God could have stopped the story there and wrapped it up. But He didn't—praise God! Instead, right before He ascended into Heaven, Jesus commissioned His disciples with a purpose: *"I have been given all authority in heaven and on earth. Therefore, go and make disciples of all the nations, baptizing them in the name of the Father and the Son and the Holy Spirit. Teach these new disciples to obey all the commands I have given you. And be sure of this: I am with you always, even to the end of the age"* (Mathew 28:19-20 NLT). His disciples did—and are still—following His last command and making disciples.

Our testimonies are examples of God's power, faithfulness, purpose, and peace; and we have the opportunity now to go and share what He has done with people of all the nations! We have the opportunity to make disciples. Praise God that the story continues and that God gives us the opportunity and purpose to go share with others the Good News of what He has done.

WE GET TO SEE HIS AMAZING HAND

Another dimension of God's great story goes beyond the opportunity to share the stories He orchestrates in our life. We also get to see what He is doing! The Lord says in Isaiah, *"For just as the heavens are higher than the earth, so my ways are higher than your ways and my thoughts higher than your thoughts"* (Isaiah 55:9 NLT). We cannot see the big picture of what God is doing all the time, but we can see the small ones that happen in our lives. Those "small" or "insignificant" testimonies of God working are not small at all—in fact, they may be playing an important role in something so big that it might blow our minds if we got to see the big picture.

Often when we look back on our lives, we see how God worked all the things we went through for good and for a much bigger purpose than we first imagined. I personally have a few of those look-backs, but I will only share one with you now.

After I accepted Jesus as my Savior and Lord, I tried to witness to people about Jesus Christ; but I just could not do it. I could take an absolutely normal person and make them hopping mad inside of thirty seconds. I was gifted! Then a friend and mentor named Tom Stebbins taught me how to witness for Jesus Christ through Evangelism Explosion, and I learned how to share Jesus with others. Praise the Lord!

I will never forget that very first night of going out on On-The-Job training (OJT). We went out into the countryside just a little bit outside Omaha, Nebraska. And I had the chance to see for the first time in my life somebody else accept Jesus. I was so afraid to be there—I had even told Tom, "You need to let me off, and I'll stand by the side of the road. You guys go on and do your thing; and then come back, pick me up, and we'll go to the church. But if I go with you, bad things are going to happen!"

Well, bad things did not happen that night. We went into a trailer home of a man who was an over-the-road trucker named Doug. If there were awards for cussing, Doug would have won them all. He could cuss between syllables! If you were to ask in that moment, "Do you think this man is going to receive Jesus?" I would have said, "No way. Absolutely not." Even his daughter and wife were so scared and skeptical by how he would react to us that they refused to even stay in the same room. They went into the kitchen and watched from there because they were sure that he was going to blow up and start throwing things at us. Well, he didn't.

Doug kept asking us questions and listened intently as we shared how Jesus came to free him from sin and have a personal relationship with him. Ever etched in my memory is this burly trucker getting down on his knees in front of his lime green, La-Z-Boy chair and accepting Jesus as Lord and Savior. When I got home, my wife asked, "Well, what'd you think? Did you like it?"

I said, "No, but I loved it—and I'm going to do this for the rest of my life if God makes me able."

So far, He has. Ann and I joined staff with Evangelism Explosion International back in 1997; and this gives me many opportunities to travel around the world, helping churches and pastors train their laypeople in how to share their faith. I am also often invited to preach in other countries.

One day I was in Jordan, which is in the Middle East. I was invited to preach in the country's second largest church. As I was preaching, I saw a young woman in the audience. Now I tend to be a bit of a long-winded preacher, but her face made me stop dead in my tracks, right in the middle of my sermon. I quickly wrapped up the sermon with the reading of a poem, shut my Bible, dismissed the congregation, and ran up the aisle. It was Doug's daughter. She had grown up in Christ, gone to Bible College, and married a young man who wanted to be a missionary. Now they were stationed in Jordan, sharing the love and truth of Christ in that needy nation.

I asked her about her dad. She told me that he had totally changed. He got involved in EE, led his mom to Christ, then started sharing with truckers all over the USA, leading hundreds, maybe thousands, to Christ. Wow. Mind boggling.

It's not often that we get to see the end of the story God is orchestrating; but in this instance, I was blessed with one of those brief looks at the beautiful, big picture of God's plan, and the part He allows us to play.

CHANGED LIVES

Changed lives—that is ultimately what we are talking about. The testimony of which brings glory to the very name of God. Our goal is to encourage God's children to learn these stories, and then to come up with a plan to share them on a regular basis as a way to get into the Gospel. What would the world look like if every believer could and would share a piece of God's story every day? That's a world I'd like to see!

ANDY'S STORY

I grew up in a family where my parents were Christians. I was brought up in a Christian environment, so knowing about God, Jesus, and the Bible was a commonplace thing; but it did not have an effect on my life. I was not a believer and that was not because I thought God did not exist. I just thought, I'm fine and everything is okay like it is. But at age 15-16, I just wanted to know why I'm here, what is the reason for me to be here. I never asked this question when I was younger. I just couldn't live with the idea that there was no reason behind my existence. So I was really looking for what is the deeper reason for my being here, being alive.

I was trying to fill my life with a lot of different things at that age. People from the small town in which I lived were telling me that it's going to take a bad end with me. I did risky things and tried to make life exciting in some way. And I thought that would bring sense into my existence, but it didn't.

So, finally, it was something very simple. Someone gave me a book as a present, and I began to read it. It was about a person who had the same feelings as I had, who went through the same things that I did, and he became a Christian. And he said, this changed everything.

I always thought that some of the people I knew who were Christians had something that I didn't have but which was exciting. But I never thought it was something that would bring satisfaction to this deep cry in my life. But I simply decided, I've tried a lot of things, now I'm going to try this.

I just started to pray. I knew how to pray, so I just started praying to Jesus knowing that He could see into my heart and He knows how I feel, and He knows my situation. I asked Him to change this, to make me a person that can see, that has a fulfilling life. A person who knows why he's there, someone whose life is significant for someone or something else.

I didn't know how it could change, but it changed a lot. It didn't change right away, it took some time. But God showed me a lot of things; where He wanted to use me and some of my skills. And He keeps on doing that until today.

After a while my longing for fulfillment got more and more quiet because it got satisfied. Today, I don't have this feeling anymore; it's just okay.

And someone who has had this same feeling knows how strong it can be. There are people that just end up in suicide because they don't find fulfillment. I don't know if I would have been at risk for that; but I guess I would have tried to do some crazy exciting thing and be killed there, rather than killing myself.

At the end of the day, it's all out of the desire to find fulfillment in life.

The only way to find real fulfillment in life is through Jesus. I've experienced it many, many times.

THREE

THE PURPOSE AND GOAL OF TESTIMONIES

WHY YOUR TESTIMONY IS SO IMPORTANT

So for the second time they called in the man who had been blind and told him, "God should get the glory for this, because we know this man Jesus is a sinner."
"I don't know whether he is a sinner," the man replied. "But I know this: I was blind, and now I can see!"

John 9:24-25 NLT

I grew up in the country where I commonly heard, "You can lead a horse to water, but you cannot make it drink!" In a way, that same kind of thinking is applied to the Gospel. How many people have heard the Gospel of Jesus Christ but just discarded the truth that they were shown? Maybe, like the horse, they just didn't want to drink?

We could dismiss our friend's, family's, and neighbor's rejection of Christ with this kind of thinking, I suppose, but the truth is that we have many reasons to believe that there just might be more to it than that. Let me see if I can explain what I mean.

When I was a boy, I was shown a little trick by an elderly farmer where he actually made a horse want to drink. How? A simple salt tablet did the trick. And that's where our testimony comes in. It's like a salt tablet!

When I come to the end of my testimony and ask, "Would you like to know how this happened?" it's not uncommon to hear the person I'm sharing with say, "Yes!" This allows the Gospel to be shared.

THE SECULAR WORLD

Before being called into Christian ministry I was in the advertising world. I owned a number of recording studios that primarily worked on creating advertisements. You know, those annoying things that go inside the program you're trying to watch. While most people turn down the audio during the commercials and turn up the audio during the show, I was always known for doing just the opposite. Weird, I know. But being in the advertising community gave me a unique perspective.

In advertising, testimonies are commonly used. Advertisers regularly utilize satisfied customers to attest to the value of their products. Television commercials pay top sports figures tens of thousands of dollars to recommend everything from deodorants to tennis shoes, beverages, and breakfast cereals. Various diet programs set forth in living color the "before and after" of their most successful clients. It's big business.

Why do they do it? Well, the answer seems obvious—because it works. People pay attention to these ads and act on them.

Now sometimes when I talk about my advertising past, people accuse me of trying to take business ideas and apply them to Christianity. In fact, I think it's the other way around. The reason why people in business do what they do is because they have learned how people respond. The business world, as a general rule, has no time for continuing to do what is ineffective.

I believe that the way people respond is not a product of the business world, or secular conditioning, but a product of how they were made by God. It's just that the business world sometimes figures it out before the church.

So we in the church should pay very close attention and learn how people respond.

LESSONS FROM SCRIPTURE

It's not only in business that we can learn the power of personal testimonies. The Scriptures contain many examples:

THE GADARENE DEMONIAC (MARK 5)

A great example of the power of a personal testimony was when Jesus healed the man filled with demons in the area of the Gadarenes, southeast of the Sea of Galilee. You remember the story?

Jesus had just sailed across the Sea of Galilee. As He stepped out onto the land, He was met by a man filled with a legion of demons. This demon-possessed man had for some time been terrorizing this area, making the people afraid to pass by his way. They had tried to chain him, but the demon-possessed man was just too strong and would always break free.

When Jesus met the man, He commanded the demons to come out of him. Normally, that worked immediately, but in this case, God had a greater plan.

It's important to note that the demons had (and have) a job to do. They were to do all that they could do to get in the way of the people believing in Jesus and hearing what He would teach them.

Another important thing to note is how the demons were under Christ's authority, just as Christ said in Matthew 28:18. They could do nothing without Christ's approval.

The man said, *"Why are you interfering with me, Jesus, Son of the Most High God? In the name of God, I beg you, don't torture me!"* (Mark 5:8 NLT).

After some conversation, they asked Jesus if He would send them out into some pigs. Christ agreed and commanded them to go. Once in the pigs, the demons drove them mad; and they raced over a cliff and drowned in the lake.

Those that were taking care of the pigs ran to tell their masters what had happened. The masters, and many of the people from the area, came out to see what had happened. When they showed up, the man that they had feared was there in his right mind, clothed, and acting normal. They became very afraid of Jesus and asked Him to leave.

The man whom Christ healed asked Jesus if he could go with Him. But Christ said, *"No, go home to your family, and tell them everything the Lord has done for you and how merciful he has been." So the man started off to visit the Ten Towns of that region and began to proclaim the great things Jesus had done for him; and everyone was amazed at what he told them* (Mark 8:19-20 NLT).

So what became of this man and his story? The Scriptures don't mention him again. But they do demonstrate what power his story had. Just a few chapters later (in Mark 8) we see that Jesus returned to the Decapolis, a region of ten cities east of the Sea of Galilee. What did He find there? Did they come out again and ask Him to leave? Quite the contrary. A great multitude came out to hear Jesus and stayed for so long that they had nothing to eat. Jesus had compassion on them and worked a great miracle—feeding over four thousand men plus their wives and children.

THE WOMAN AT THE WELL (JOHN 4)

In this well known story, Jesus meets a Samaritan woman at Jacob's well and asks her for a drink. It starts quite a discussion in which Christ shares the Gospel with her.

As an EE'er, I find it interesting that He basically follows the EE outline (Grace, Man, God, Christ, Faith)!

In the process, Jesus tells her quite a bit about herself, including how many husbands she has had, and the fact that the man that she currently lived with was not her husband. She was amazed. He then tells her that He is the Christ (Messiah).

When the disciples come back from the city, the woman hurries off and tells the towns people what she has seen and heard. She says, *"Come and see a man who told me everything I ever did! Could he possibly be the Messiah?"* (John 4:29 NLT).

The whole town came because of her testimony of Jesus. First they believed because of what she said about Jesus, but when they heard Him, they believed He was the Christ. Because of her testimony a whole town was saved!

THE MAN HEALED OF BLINDNESS (JOHN 9)

As Jesus passes by, He meets a man that has been blind since birth. With great compassion, Jesus heals the man by spitting on the ground, making some mud, and covering the blind man's eyes with it. Jesus then tells him to go wash in the pool of Siloam. When he did, his sight was given to him.

As neighbors noticed, they began to question him as to how this happened. He said, *"The man they call Jesus made mud and spread it over my eyes and told me, 'Go to the pool of Siloam and wash yourself.' So I went and washed, and now I can see!"* (John 9:11 NLT).

The man's telling of his testimony eventually got him called before the Pharisees, who questioned him as a hostile witness. His parents also had to testify. When called again, this poor, formerly blind, most likely uneducated man got the chance to preach to the Jewish leaders a powerful message. Offended and outraged that he was giving Jesus, who they called a "sinner," credit for his miraculous recovery of sight, the Pharisees pressed the man hard to give God the glory for what had happened.

"I don't know whether he is a sinner," the man replied. *"But I know this: I was blind, and now I can see!"* (v. 25).

Unable to deny what had happened, the offended and angry leaders tossed him out.

This story proves that we don't have to be expert witnesses. We just need to be ready to tell others what Jesus has done for us. The story will open doors.

THE APOSTLE PAUL (ACTS 22)

Our final testimony in this chapter is that of Saul of Tarsus, more commonly known as the Apostle Paul. In Acts 22, we find Paul before the Jews in Jerusalem. He tells them the story of how he used to be a zealous persecutor of the Way (v. 4). On his way to Damascus, a great light appeared to him, blinding his eyes. It was Jesus of Nazareth, the one whom he was persecuting. Jesus called him to serve Him. In verses 14 and 15 Paul is told, *"The God of our ancestors has chosen you to know his will and to see the Righteous One and hear him speak. For you are to be his witness, telling everyone what you have seen and heard."*

And that is what Paul did. For the rest of his days. Against great adversity, ultimately leading to his death, he served Jesus. In the process, he wrote most of the New Testament, and began an outreach to the Gentiles that has reached around the world. If one wants to disprove the truth of Christianity, they would have to disprove the conversion of Saul. A changed life is the key to the story of Christ in us, too.

Notice that he set forth the three essential elements of a good testimony:

1. What I was before I received eternal life (vv. 3-5)
2. How I received eternal life (vv. 6-11)
3. What eternal life meant to me (vv. 12-21).

BOTTOM LINE

In each case above, we see the power of the testimony God gave to them. In the sharing of this truth, men and woman were encouraged to stop and consider what God was doing. These testimonies by the Gadarene, the Samaritan woman, the man born blind, and Paul, were the "salt tablet" that made the others want to drink.

The purpose and goal of a testimony is to cause those you come in contact with to want to hear the Gospel. It is not our stories that change people's lives. We are not trying to inspire them the live better. For only the Gospel is the "power of God unto salvation." Our testimonies are not self-help mumbo-jumbo, but proof of an alive God who is active in the affairs of men. So then, the purpose is to shine light on the faithfulness of God in our lives. And our goal is for the Gospel to be heard.

When used correctly, the story God has enacted in you will lead people to stop and say, "I'd like to hear how that happened!"

Rhonda's Story

I was in year twelve at school, so I was 17 years old. My family had sent me along to Sunday school as they were not church attenders themselves. As I got into high school, I started to wonder what you could really believe. I was wanting to know, "Is it true or not?" Or is it just make-believe "Santa Claus" stuff? I was going off to university the next year, so I really wanted to know. Somehow I figured it made a difference in your life.

I went to bed every night for several months and prayed to God saying, "If you're there, please show me." But nothing happened.

Which wasn't very helpful, because it could be that it meant that He wasn't there, or if He was there it meant that He didn't want to talk to me.

In the meantime, a friend of mine invited me along to hear a speaker who was visiting our hometown. His name was Billy Graham. I had seen that he'd been in Sydney a few weeks before. On the front page of the newspaper, an aerial shot showed thousands of people herding in to listen to this man speak. They filled a stadium!

I was on the school debating team and so when my friend asked me to go I thought, "You could learn a lot about public speaking from a man like that." So I said, "Yes!"

I went along, but little did I know that God was in the process of answering my prayer.

Billy Graham spoke and just kept saying, "The Bible says...the Bible says..." There was a sense of certainty and authority about what he said. It was really quite compelling.

I watched people begin to go forward while I sat there watching. My friend turned to me and said, "Would you like to go down?" I replied, "Yes, please!"

Of course, I thought she was going to go, too. She took me down and handed me over to a counselor, who took my details and prayed with me. I was certainly overwhelmed by the whole event.

A little later in the month, I got an invitation in the mail to go to a Christian camp. Miraculously, my parents paid for my way to go. My journey with Christ started, and I've grown in my faith ever since.

What started with a prayer that God was prompting me to pray, and that He was answering, has led to the wonderful changes in my life.

I love the fact that everyone, no matter what personality or capacity, can respond to the Gospel. No one will ever exhaust the riches of God's truth.

In this walk with God, I have gathered a sense of certainty, confidence, direction and purpose. I began to really understand the Bible, and that has given my life real confidence and meaning.

FOUR

DISCOVERING YOUR STORY

LEARNING TO SEE THE GOD STORIES IN YOUR LIFE

---

*Therefore, if anyone is in Christ, he is a new creation; old things
have passed away; behold, all things have become new.*

2 Corinthians 5:16 NLT

---

*Note: This chapter largely comes from training materials produced by Evangelism
Explosion International. When you see the word "prospect", we are referring to the
person that you are desiring to share the Gospel with, because the goal of the testimony is getting into the Gospel with our friends, relatives, work associates, and
neighbors. You will see a lot of references to how the testimony works within our
sharing the Gospel in our day-to-day lives, as well as within training situations.*

I HAVE BEEN A CHRISTIAN MY WHOLE LIFE

*I was raised in a Christian family and was taught
the Word of God from a young age. Since coming here
[to Fiji], I have learned many things about my life.
When I hear other testimonies from people who have*

passed through many difficult things, I am very grateful that I did not pass through similar situations. I used to think that 'big' testimonies were only stories of big change, but now I understand that my life is a big testimony too because God has protected me from passing through those difficult situations. And there still was a change inside of me. When I was little, I wasn't sure if I was going to Heaven or not; and it was a fear in my life. But then I understood all that Jesus did for me; and because of my family and church, I already knew all the stories in the Bible about Jesus. On that day when I was young, I understood that Jesus came and died to cleanse my sin. Now I can live in peace and am very grateful for what Jesus did for me.

-Christian, an intern from Mexico

Many Christians have a similar testimony to Christian's story. They grew up in a Christian household, knew Christ at a young age, and have been living faithfully for Him ever since. There have rarely been horrible situations in their life or they have not had extreme struggles with sin to overcome. Because they do not have a testimony of a big change from evil to good, they often think that their testimony does not have any power to it. This is not so at all! Every testimony has the power of the

Holy Spirit, who has come into each of our hearts as Christians and changed us from the inside out. The Holy Spirit convicts and changes hearts in huge ways, but the Spirit also can change and mend hearts in subtle ways.

In John 3, the Bible talks about how Nicodemus came to Jesus to ask to see the kingdom of God. Nicodemus was a devout man and had sought after God his entire life. He spent his life trying to learn about God, serve God, and seek His face. Even though Nicodemus was a "good man," Jesus still answers him with, *"Most assuredly, I say to you, unless one is born again, he cannot see the kingdom of God"* (John 3:3 NKJV). Regardless of whether or not we grew up in church with a Christian family surrounding us or if we grew up in a broken family who has never heard about God, we must be born again and ask the Holy Spirit to come into our hearts for us to be a "new creation." The Bible says in 2 Corinthians 5:17-19 NKJV:

> *Therefore, if anyone is in Christ, he is a new creation; old things have passed away; behold, all things have become new. Now all things are of God, who has reconciled us to Himself through Jesus Christ, and has given us the ministry of reconciliation, that is, that God was in Christ reconciling the world to Himself, not imputing their trespasses to them, and has committed to us the word of reconciliation.*

Our testimony is us simply testifying to the fact that God has *"reconciled us to Himself through Jesus Christ."* Whether we have a story that tells of a huge change where God literally plucked us straight out of hell on earth or a story that tells of His faithfulness through changing our lives at a young age, we are still to testify about our reconciliation to Him. Now that we have been changed, our purpose that God has committed to us is to spread the word of reconciliation through our story.

WHERE DO YOU START?

A testimony may take either of two forms. It may be a church testimony, or it may be a personal testimony—your own or that of another. In the beginning of your Gospel adventure, it may be easiest to start with the church testimony while you look for and develop your personal testimony. If you are part of a organized calling program at your church (like Evangelism Explosion), you will want to know and be able to share the church testimony in addition to your personal testimony.

CHURCH TESTIMONY

A church testimony is used in order to establish the mission of the church, i.e., to proclaim the Gospel that men and women may have eternal life. It also precludes the objection, "I want eternal life, but I don't want to go to church."

The purpose of this testimony is to lead easily into the first diagnostic question (and thus the Gospel) and to get them to admit that they do not have the assurance of eternal life, if indeed they do not. This, of course, is best used with those who have visited your church. After asking if they have any questions about the new church they have just visited, and answering them quickly, proceed as follows with a church testimony.

"Well then, let me tell you a little bit about our church. Christ came into the world, as you may know, in order that people might have life—that they might have it abundantly and they might have it eternally. And yet we have found that there are millions of people in this country, people who attend church regularly, try to live a good life, and follow the teachings of Christ, and yet somehow the church has failed to communicate to them how they can know for sure that they have eternal life and are going to go to Heaven.

"How about you, Mary [or John], have you come to the place in your spiritual life where you know for certain that if you were to die tonight you would go to Heaven, or is that something you would say you're still working on?"

This simple church testimony leads right into the first diagnostic question and puts them in a position to be willing to answer it honestly.

PERSONAL TESTIMONY

To be an effective witness for our Savior, the first tool needed is a clear, forceful personal testimony. It is the most original contribution toward an effective witness and the first thing shared because it is familiar and is the thing easiest to share. It also creates a desire to hear the Gospel. Christians are the "salt of the earth," and their salty testimonies can make non-Christians thirsty for the Water of Life.

If you have met God in Jesus Christ in your own life, you have found Him working according to His promises. Your experience of God's faithfulness is the substance of your testimony. As you prepare your testimony, realize that you are fashioning an evangelistic tool so you will be a more proficient witness.

Some Christians give admirable testimonies—testimonies with zip and life—testimonies devoid of rough spots and trite platitudes. However, others stumble and bumble in a disorganized, uninteresting, ineffectual manner. We must sharpen our tools and learn to use them effectively.

Scripture says, *"And this is the testimony: that God has given us eternal life, and this life is in His Son. He who has the Son has life; he who does not have the Son of God does not have life"* (1 John 5:11-12 NKJV). We are dealing now with the proper use of personal testimony as an evangelistic tool.

Throughout this section we will use the phrase "eternal life" as equivalent to "trusting Christ" or "becoming a Christian." If you use the name of Christ repeatedly in your testimony, you will find that it often programs your prospect so that his answer to the second diagnostic question does not truly reflect his own relationship to Christ (if you need to be reminded of the questions being spoken of here, look again to the top of page 9). The word Christian is such a highly connotative word that using it in the testimony can also generate difficulties.

Giving a personal testimony—simply telling what eternal life has meant to you—is the first aspect of witnessing. Now, if you cannot tell someone that Christ has saved you, you are not an evangelist; you are an evangelistic field, and you need an evangelist to lead you to conversion.

This is not to say you must know when you were converted. However, you must know if you have been converted. Many people don't know when they became Christians. One of the great preachers of a past generation, Dr. Peter Eldersveld, said he could remember clearly when he was three years old, and he knew that at that time he trusted in the blood of Jesus Christ alone for his salvation. He was well taught by his parents and came to a very early faith and could remember nothing else.

In order to witness for Christ, you must have the assurance that you have eternal life and know that Christ Jesus is your Savior.

MOTIVES FOR RECEIVING ETERNAL LIFE

When we refer to "eternal life," we mean more than the everlasting life we will spend with God in Heaven. Jesus said in John 10:10, *"I have come that they may have life, and that they may have it more abundantly."* And in John 17:3, He added, *"And this is eternal life, that they may know You, the only true God, and Jesus Christ whom You have sent."*

Hence, eternal life has two dimensions: the abundant life of knowing God on this earth and the everlasting life of growing to know Him even better throughout eternity in Heaven.

Your testimony starts with the first dimension and points to the blessings of knowing Christ in the here and now, such as fellowship, love, forgiveness, freedom from fear, etc. It concludes with a statement that you know for sure that when you die you will go to be with God in Heaven.

Let us now consider some of the blessings which may well meet the needs of the prospect and motivate him to receive eternal life:

1. **Fellowship.** Christ provides us with Christian fellowship and friends. Why do unsaved people attend church? The answer: friendliness. Friendliness is significant to people because they are lonely. A basic human need is friendship. When people hear that God creates a fellowship, they find this meaningful.

2. **Love.** God fills us with His love. Our homes in America have every luxury conceivable. However, many lack the essential ingredient of love. Strife and jealousy lurk in gadget-filled rooms, and many marriages are little better than an armed truce.

3. **People long to be loved.** A testimony to the love that God brings into a life and a home may awaken your prospect to a need that has not been met for years.

4. **Forgiveness.** God forgives us and relieves us of our sense of guilt. A major problem people are unable to cope with is guilt. Guilt fills our psychiatric hospitals, for it fractures the

human personality. It causes anxiety and depression. It creates havoc in the human heart. The greatest picture of relief from guilt is in John Bunyan's allegory, Pilgrim's Progress. As Christian kneels at the cross, the burden of guilt falls off and rolls into the empty tomb, never to be seen again. The burden of guilt is lifted at Calvary.

5. **A friend in my trouble.** Christ is a friend to lean upon in trouble. He imparts strength to the discouraged, the worn down, and the defeated. It has been charged that Christ is a crutch. How do you answer that? "That's fine. I'm a cripple. I need a crutch."

6. **Adoption.** He adopts us into His family. *"God sets the solitary in families"* (Psalm 68:6 NKJV). God is our Father, and we are brothers and sisters in Christ. Frequently we say to a person who has just accepted Christ, "Welcome into the family of God. I have discovered something. We are related. You and I are brothers and sisters, and we are members of the greatest family on earth: God's family."

7. **New perspectives.** He gives a whole new perspective on life. One of the most devastating questions you can ask anybody is "What are you living for?" Most people have no idea. When one becomes a Christian, all this is changed. We are given a clarity and perspective unknowable to the

non-Christian. The enigmas of the universe, the questions that perplex people, begin to fall into place, and we begin to see the puzzle of life more clearly.

8. **Freedom from fear.** He delivers us from the fears of living and dying. Many people are fearful. Some will say they are not afraid of hell, but they are afraid to take the garbage out at night.

ESSENTIAL QUALITIES OF AN EFFECTIVE PERSONAL TESTIMONY

1. **Emphasize the positive.** One of the common errors in giving a testimony is to belabor the "before" and minimize the "after." Just the opposite should be our method. You do not help people by giving them a tedious life history. They have no particular interest in where you attended school, where your parents live, or when you moved from here to there. Rather, do as Jesus commanded the demoniac: *"Go...and tell how great things the Lord hath done for thee."* Emphasize the positive benefits.

Dr. Kennedy took teams out every week to teach them to witness. He did this for years, throughout his entire ministry. One day, he had a Christian who accompanied him on an evangelistic call. Dr. Kennedy requested that the man give a testimony, to which he said, "When I accepted

Christ, I lost all my friends. They wouldn't have anything to do with me. Then I lost my job. You know, all the people who do worldly things (and he mentioned half a dozen things that evidently thrilled the people they were visiting) stop being your friend when you give up these worldly practices." It was as if he had given a five-minute discourse on why one should not become a Christian! It seems that many Christians are about as effective when they tell why a person ought to become a Christian. Emphasize the positive benefits of having eternal life.

2. **Identify with the people you imagine you will be sharing with.** While you are just beginning to write your personal testimony, the truth is that you will likely have multiple testimonies of what God has done in your life. Everyday, God does amazing things in our life, and we need to start to look for these things and be prepared to share them with others.

As you share with your friends, family, work associates, and neighbors, you want them to be able to identify with you. By "identify," I mean that you need to select truthful statements about yourself that will help them see themselves in you. As has been said earlier, the use of personal testimony helps to preclude the objection raised when the prospect is asked questions about his spiritual life that are personal.

In the conversation, you will likely have gained enough insight to determine whether your prospect is self-righteous, indifferent, a libertine, an agnostic, etc. If, for example, you discover your prospect to be a self-righteous intellectual who is caring for his elderly parents, you would make a fatal mistake by saying, "My parents did not do right by me. They did not give me any religious instruction, and their reprobate lives led me to become a wretched character. I embezzled my employer's funds and was un-faithful to my wife. Then I met Christ." Your prospect would think, "Good, you needed Him, but I don't!" And he would start watching his silverware in case you had a spiri-tual relapse.

How much better to say to your pharisaical philosopher: "I never gave any thought to the reason I was here in the world until one day when such and such happened. Oh, I knew there was a Heaven, but I never gave much thought about how I could get there." It does no good to tell a very righteous person what a great criminal you were. Instead, tell him the aspects of your life that were similar to the life of your prospect. You thereby let him know that you were the same as he is. Then, when you tell him that you found something very vital was missing from your life, he will sense something is lacking in his life. If we give a strong statement of our certainty of eternal life and the fantastic value of that assurance, this will act as a logical stepping-stone into the first diagnostic question.

3. **Do not give answers before you ask questions.** As we present the Gospel with our friend, it should have certain elements of mystery. You confront the prospect with a problem in a manner that identifies him/her with the problem. As you let him/her see and feel the problem, the suspense mounts and he/she gets into the problem; then you solve the problem by presenting Christ in the Gospel. However, you do not want to give any answers to the questions you will ask later.

Suppose you were witnessing to John, and Barbara is your companion on the visit. Before you establish what John is trusting in for his salvation, you ask Barbara to give her testimony. She says, "The pastor came to see me and asked me why I thought I should go to Heaven. I didn't know I needed to trust only in Christ, so I told him I hoped I was good enough to get in. I went to church every Sunday, helped needy people at Christmas, and never intentionally hurt anyone. But the pastor told me I could never get to Heaven that way because I was a sinner and needed the cleansing blood of Jesus Christ. So I stopped trusting what I was doing and started trusting Christ's work on the cross for me."

Now you turn to John and ask, "John, what are you trusting in for eternal life?" His certain reply will be, "I am trusting in the blood of Christ." He may not have the slightest idea about why Christ's blood avails for anything, or what is involved in the act of trusting Him for salvation; he is just parroting the "right answer" he heard Barbara give in her testimony.

If the testimony is used during the "introduction of the Gospel" (as part of an Evangelism Explosion local church training), speak in general terms as you tell how you received eternal life. That is, tell what your life was like before, and then say something like this: "And then I received eternal life and everything was changed." Go on to tell of the changes in your life. It will be noted that you have not told them anything about how you received eternal life or that it was a gift received by faith.

If, however, the testimony is all you have time for, you must make especially clear just how you passed from death unto life.

4. **Be specific.** You must not generalize or you will lose your audience. To be effective, you must be specific. You can say, "It is wonderful!" What, exactly, is wonderful? Or you may say, "I have peace." Exactly what do you mean? In what way do you have peace? Be specific—make your testimony concrete.

"It is wonderful to know when I lay my head on my pillow tonight that if I do not awaken in bed in the morning, I will awaken in paradise with God."

"I had a Christian son killed in Iraq, yet my heart is filled with peace because I know he has eternal life. Even though he was killed by an enemy mortar, he has a home now in Heaven, and one day we'll be reunited there."

People remember specifics. They forget generalities. What are some points we might make in sharing what eternal life means to us?

5. **Avoid cliché.** Christian jargon is meaningless to the non-Christian. Clichés jangle unbelieving ears. For example: "Receive Christ, and you'll receive a blessing." This is so common to us, but the non-Christian will cringe at the thought of receiving a blessing. What is it to receive a blessing? How does it come, by mail? Or does it fall from the sky? We must always distinguish the connotation from

the denotation of a word. The denotation is what the word actually means according to Webster or a theological dictionary. For example, the word "evangelism" is undoubtedly, by derivation, one of the most beautiful words in our language. It comes from the word evangel, which means "good angel," and it is the glad tidings. Nothing could be more beautiful.

However, what does evangelism connote to some people? It stirs up images of people on the street corners beating drums, shouting, and doing all sorts of unpleasant things. The connotations of a word are the barnacles it picks up as it sails the sea of life.

6. **Use direct and indirect quotations.** Quotations arouse interest.

7. **Avoid giving a travelogue.** Details about when and where you lived or traveled decrease interest, deal with externals, and miss the real spiritual matters you want to share.

8. **Focus on God's faithfulness.** Details about your sinfulness or backsliding also detract from your objective of pointing the person to God and His grace in your life.

9. **Use humor constructively.** If the situation becomes tense, you can relieve the tension by saying something comical. But avoid a frivolous attitude toward the Gospel.

10. **Speak pictorially.** "I was in bed, and the Gospel came on the clock radio. Fortunately it was out of my reach, so I couldn't just roll over and turn it off. I got out of bed, and just about the time I got to the radio..." Here is a situation people can visualize. If they are not seeing in their minds the thing you are talking about, they are probably seeing something personal they are thinking about, rather than listening to you.

ADULT CONVERSION TESTIMONY

To apply the above suggestions, you will generally find it practical and helpful to write out your testimony before you give it. The length should be about three hundred words. If you were converted at an age when you remember graphically the details before and after your conversion, you will want to include the following three essential elements in writing your own personal testimony:

1. What I was before I received eternal life
2. How I received eternal life
3. What eternal life has meant to me

Let us now consider each part of the adult conversion testimony to see how it can be made meaningful to others.

WHAT I WAS BEFORE

Select one life concept such as loneliness, strife, guilt, fear of death, emptiness, rejection, insecurity, depression. Then include it (only one concept per testimony) in an opening statement, saying, "Before I received eternal life, my life was filled with a paralyzing fear of death."

Next, move from the general statement to a specific illustration out of your own life experiences. Give concrete details to make your illustration come alive. People remember specifics but forget generalities. For instance, you may want to say something like, "When I was in college, I was living in a small mobile home. One night a terrible storm arose with wind gusts over fifty miles an hour! The wind was so strong that the rain was blowing horizontally across the ground. Our little mobile home was rocking on its concrete-block foundation, and a bolt of lightning struck a tall oak tree right next to it. I was really frightened and sat on the edge of the sofa fearful that I was going to die."

HOW I RECEIVED ETERNAL LIFE

At this point, you may want to say something like, "Not many months later, a friend shared with me the most wonderful news I'd ever heard—that God had provided eternal life for me and what the conditions were to receive that life. As a result, many things have changed in my life."

Notice, you did not give away the answers to the two diagnostic questions you are about to ask.

WHAT ETERNAL LIFE HAS MEANT TO ME

At this point, you may want to share the life concept in reverse. If you selected fear of death as your life concept, you will now want to speak of courage in the face of death. If you chose the concept of guilt, you may now want to speak of forgiveness. The reverse of depression is hope; of emptiness, purpose; of rebellion, obedience, etc.

Then you will want to illustrate the reverse life concept with another illustration from your experience.

For instance, you may want to say, "The fear of death is now gone, and in its place is courage when facing death situations or thoughts about death. Not long after I received eternal life we were driving north on an interstate during an ice storm that put a sheet of glazed ice on the highway," etc. Go on to describe in detail your close call with death. Then conclude, "God gave me complete peace in the knowledge that if death came, it could only usher me into His Heaven! What a difference it makes knowing that I have eternal life. And it's the same today. I know that if I were to die right now, I would go to be with God in Heaven. May I ask you a question?"

Your testimony regarding eternal life leads naturally into the Gospel.

Now you can shape, sharpen, smooth, and perfect your personal testimony and fulfill the admonition of the apostle Peter: *"Always be ready to give a defense to everyone who asks you a reason for the hope that is in you, with meekness and fear;"* (1 Peter 3:15 NKJV). Go over your testimony, and get rid of the rough spots. Eliminate the trite sayings. Get zip and life into it, and then ask God to help you use it. In three minutes you should be able to effectively tell what you were before receiving eternal life, how you received it, and what it has meant in your life.

CHILDHOOD CONVERSION TESTIMONY

There are some Christians who have no recollection of when or how they became Christians. They received Christ at such an early age, they do not remember ever not being a Christian. How will these people give a testimony?

Whether they remember it or not, we know how they became Christians. They came to understand that they were sinners in the sight of God. They came to realize that God loved them and that Christ died for their sins. They came to trust in

Him for their salvation and to receive Him as Lord and Master of their lives. How do we know that is the way they became Christians? Because that is the only way anyone becomes a Christian. Whether this happens in an emotionally packed hour in an evangelistic crusade, or gradually when the person is two, three, four, or five years old, every Christian has come to understand those things and to trust in Jesus Christ.

However, the important things to emphasize are the benefits that eternal life has brought. This is especially important for the person reared in a Christian home and church whose lifestyle has not drastically changed. Internal feelings, purposes, and motives have been changed by Christ, and these things should be emphasized.

OTHER THOUGHTS

A Christian who has backslidden drastically and then returned to a closer fellowship with Christ need not include this in their testimony, since the introduction of this whole new area will only serve to confuse the person to whom you are speaking.

Under normal circumstances, you should share your testimony before you share the Gospel. But sometimes, in order to heighten your friends's interest, you may share it just before you ask if they want to receive the gift of eternal life.

When doing questionnaire evangelism, share it after the questions and just before your Gospel presentation.

Remember, in any case, if the prospect becomes resistant, you should always personalize your presentation of the Gospel. The best way to do that is to weave your personal experience (i.e., your personal testimony) into your presentation. People will argue doctrine till the blood runs, but they cannot argue with your personal testimony.

In the next chapter, you'll have the chance to begin to develop your first of many testimonies. Pray that God will use your story to see many people come to faith in Christ.

NAKITI'S STORY
FIJI

W hen we faced struggles, my wife would say, "Why don't you try Jesus?" And I always wondered, where do these ideas come from? Then one Sunday, she asked me to go with her to church. I really didn't want to go but because my wife asked me, and it was a rainy day, I went with her to the service.

During the church service, the preacher came down from the pulpit, and for the first time ever, I heard a preacher say, "This morning, God spoke to me." And I thought, "What? I thought God only spoke to the prophets in the Bible."

That morning was the first time for me ever to hear somebody say, "God spoke to me." I suppose it really made me want to listen to what he was saying.

He preached about hell and eternity, eternal life. And to conclude his sermon, he was saying, "There is no choice. After this life, there are only two places. Either you're going to Heaven with Jesus or you're going to hell and spend eternity with the devil."

From that day, I surrendered my life to God. I just walked up. The preaching had not yet finished. But I just walked up the aisle and knelt down and surrendered my life to Jesus. And that was the amazing thing. It was the fourth of August, 1991, which is also my birthday.

It was really hard starting for me because I was born in a culturally Christian family. My mom and dad are both Christians, but they were not very serious about their relationship. So coming to be a "born-again" Christian in a so-called Christian home is really hard. I choose the way that every other family member didn't like, you know? Because I was not sitting down and spending the night drinking with them, things began to change. After a few months, the whole family had turned their back on us.

Even my dad said to me, "Don't call me your dad, you are out from the family." And all my family did the same thing. "We are not your brothers anymore. We are not your sisters anymore."

After a few years, things started to get better. They saw the real change that had happened in us. One day, my dad came up to where we were in the outer island. I was working in the government at the time. My dad was really, really frustrated with me. We had not talked for so many years. He made a point to come and visit us. The reason he came was that he wanted to find out what kind of belief or faith that we had.

The day he came, he just showed up without telling us he was coming. So there he was in our house on the island. He stayed four days with us without saying very much.

Then one morning we woke up, had breakfast, and I asked him to say grace for our food. I found that he was in tears, and I asked him, "What happened? Is there anything wrong?" Slowly he said to us, "I came to investigate what kind of God or what kind of religion you're in. Now I can see, because of the way you live, I know who God is. So I can go home a happy man. I can tell the entire family how you live life in your faith with God."

Then he told all the family members. The family members called me and said, "Nakiti, we want you back. Please come and share with us." And the next year, the whole family came for Christmas, with the exception of one of my brothers. Six of my brothers, their wives, and their children, came to our house.

During that week, they asked me if I would do devotions every morning and evening. They stayed with us for two weeks.

One Sunday, I did the whole EE Gospel presentation, and everybody said, "Yes, we want to receive Christ!"

We know first hand how God can heal relationships. Our job is to be faithful to His calling in our lives, and He will give us the delight of our hearts.

FIVE

PREPARING YOUR STORY

SHARING THE LIFE THAT CHRIST HAS GIVEN YOU

When He comes, in that Day, to be glorified in His saints and to be admired among all those who believe, because our testimony among you was believed.

2 Thessalonians 1:10 NKJV

I n this chapter, you'll have the chance to write out your testimony to share with others as God gives you opportunity. This will likely be just the first of many stories that you will use in your life. This process can be repeated as you identify other areas where God has brought about a stark change in you.

ADULT CONVERSION TESTIMONIES

If you came to Christ as an adult, start by stating a negative concept of what you were like before you received eternal life.

An example might be, "Before I received eternal life, I was afraid of death." Some other negative concepts might be:

- ☐ loneliness
- ☐ guilt
- ☐ strife
- ☐ purposelessness
- ☐ depression
- ☐ rebellion
- ☐ emptiness
- ☐ insecurity
- ☐ rejection
- ☐ fear of failure
- ☐ weakness

Which one seems to fit your story best?

Next, illustrate that concept with a graphic anecdote or example out of your experience before you received eternal life. Make sure to use picturesque language so people can visualize the concept.

Here's an example: "I was aboard a troop transport at sea. Screeching sirens warned that our vessel was sinking. Petrified with fear, I put on my life jacket and searched frantically for a lifeboat. It turned out to be only a fire drill but that awful fear of death continued to haunt me until one day..."

Then, state that you received eternal life. If you are planning to share the Gospel with the person you're sharing your testimony with, then make sure to leave out the details of your conversion experience. If you were very young when you came to Christ, it's usually a good idea to leave out your age as well, as many will think it was a childish idea. Try to use "eternal life" as synonymous for receiving Christ, being born-again, accepting Christ into your heart, etc., as it keeps your theme consistent and avoids some common misconceptions.

Next, state in one sentence and with one positive concept what you are like since you received eternal life. An example might be, "Now that I have eternal life I have courage in the face of death."

The positive concept should be the opposite of the negative one you experienced before you received eternal life. Some other positive concepts might be:

- ☐ friendliness
- ☐ forgiveness
- ☐ peace
- ☐ purpose
- ☐ obedience
- ☐ love
- ☐ freedom

☐ fulfillment

☐ hope

☐ security

☐ acceptance

☐ strength

Then, illustrate that positive concept with another graphic anecdote or example out of your life since you received Christ. Make sure to use picturesque language so people can visualize the concept. Again, an example, "I was driving during an ice storm. Semi-trailer trucks surrounded me. A strong wind caused my car to begin spinning. The possibility of death became very real, yet God had given me a deep peace that I knew if I were to die, I would go to Heaven."

Always conclude by stating that you know for sure that you have eternal life and are going to Heaven when you die. Example: "The best thing of all is that I know today if I were to die, I'd go straight to Heaven." That allows you to transition into the Gospel by asking permission to ask a question: "May I ask you a question?"

- It's appropriate to ask them if they have eternal life because you just told them that you do.

- But because the subject is so personal and for some people very private, you should ask permission to ask about it.

IF CONVERTED AS A CHILD

Whether you were converted at age 40 or 4, there are two crucial issues: Do you know you have eternal life, and are you trusting in Jesus Christ for eternal life?

It's best not to start by saying you were converted as a child because adults can't identify with childhood conversions. Simply state, "I'm glad I know I have eternal life because..." Then follow the same instructions given previously for the second half of the adult testimony.

Here's an example: "I'm glad I have eternal life because it gives me peace in the face of death. I was driving during an ice storm, etc,..."

Some points to remember in preparing your testimony:

1. Emphasize the positive.

   - The focus is God's faithfulness not our sinfulness.
   - Don't over-stress the "before" section or your testimony will become exaggerated, like the "Hulk"!
   - Don't highlight what you gave up or lost, but what you gained.

- Underscore the positive benefits of abundant life here and now.

- Select and insert appropriate humor to relax prospects.

2. Where possible, identify with your prospects.

  - Select truthful statements about yourself that will help prospects see themselves in you.

  - You will have to listen carefully and remember what the prospects shared earlier.

3. Avoid using words commonly used in church but not understood by non-Christians such as "hallelujah," "born again," or "altar."

4. Write your testimony in about 300 words, to be spoken in no more than 3 minutes, using the models and work sheets on the following pages.

SAMPLE TESTIMONIES

ADULT CONVERSION TESTIMONY

Before I received eternal life, I had a fear of death and dying. The thought of death terrified me because I had no idea what lay beyond death's door for me. When I was in college, I was living in a small mobile home. One night a terrible storm arose with wind gusts over 50 miles an hour! The wind was so strong that the rain was blowing horizontally across the ground. Our little mobile home was rocking on its concrete block foundation, and a bolt of lightening struck a tall oak tree right next to it. I was frightened and sat on the edge of the sofa fearful that I was going to die.

Not many months later, a friend shared with me something very wonderful; and I received eternal life. Many things changed in my life.

Now that I have eternal life, the fear of death and dying is gone. Not long after I had received eternal life, we were driving north on Interstate 57 during an ice storm that put a sheet of glazed ice on the highway. We were easing along at 25 miles an hour when we came alongside a semi-trailer truck. The wind was blowing very hard, and the trailer began to act like a sail catching the wind. The truck was gradually being pushed across the center line and steadily toward our car. There was nowhere to go! We could not go to the right; the truck was there. If we had gone to the left, it would have been to the ditch with the possibility of that truck on top of us! As we waited to see the outcome, death or tragic injury seemed certain. My whole life panned before me; and yet God gave me complete peace in my heart knowing that even in light of this almost certain tragedy, I knew for certain that if I were to die, I would go to Heaven. What a joy and difference that made as I faced that danger. And it's the same today. I know that if I were to die right now, I would go to be with God in Heaven.

May I ask you a question?

CHILDHOOD CONVERSION TESTIMONY

I'm glad that I have eternal life, because it has given me the certainty of knowing where I'm going when I die.

Not long ago we were driving north on Interstate 57 during an ice storm that put a sheet of glazed ice on the highway. We were easing along at 25 miles an hour looking for a place to get off the highway to find shelter for the night. As we were driving, we came alongside a semi-trailer truck. The wind was blowing very hard and the trailer truck became like a sailboat catching the wind. The truck was gradually being pushed across the center line and steadily toward our car.

There was nowhere to go. We couldn't go to the right as we would run into the truck; we couldn't go to the left because we would eventually end up in a ditch with the truck on top of us! As we waited to see the outcome, death or tragic injury seemed certain. My whole life panned before me; and yet God gave me complete peace in the my heart knowing that even in light of this almost certain tragedy, I knew for certain that if I were to die I would go to Heaven. What a joy and difference that made as I faced that danger. And it's the same today. I know that if I were to die right now, I would go to be with God in Heaven.

May I ask you a question?

PERSONAL TESTIMONY WORKSHEET

(For use if converted as an adult)

I. Before I received eternal life ...

A. State one life concept (i.e., worry, fear of death, lack of purpose).

B. Illustrate this concept with specific examples(s) from your own life (use pictorial or descriptive language).

II. Then I received eternal life.

III. Now that I have eternal life ...

    A. State the reverse of concept I-A above (how God completed your life with peace, freedom from fear, or purpose).

    B. Give reverse illustration of I-B above from your own life (use descriptive language).

    C. Always include the statement that you know you have eternal life and that you are going to Heaven when you die.

    D. Transition: "May I ask you a question?"

PERSONAL TESTIMONY WORKSHEET

(For use if converted in childhood)

I. I'm glad I know that I have eternal life because ...

A. State one positive life concept (i.e., peace, security, purpose).

B. Illustrate this concept with a specific example from your own life (use pictorial or descriptive language).

C. Always include a statement that you know that you have eternal life and that you are going to Heaven when you die.

D. Transition: "May I ask you a question?"

Refining Your Testimony

After you have written a first draft of your personal testimony, it will be necessary to have it reviewed by someone else. Pray, asking God for a teachable spirit, realizing you may never have prepared your testimony with the same intentions and restrictions required for a "before-the-Gospel" testimony. Keep in mind that testimonies are very personal and unique in nature. They are not difficult to write but to be meaningful do require some creative thought.

- Writing styles vary from person to person.
- No two testimonies are alike.
- Spelling and penmanship are not the focus.

Ask a friend to review your testimony. Here's a list of what they are to look for as they read it. Did it:

- Express the positive benefits of having eternal life?
- Give away the answer to the second diagnostic question?
- Use picturesque language?
- Include needless travelogue or extraneous material?
- Avoid Christian "clichés" and vague generalities?
- Express God's faithfulness?
- Use constructive humor, but avoid being frivolous?
- Illustrate with specific examples from your experience?
- Express assurance that you have eternal life?

If you are able to work with a group of people at church that are all developing testimonies, then each person in the group should read aloud his/her testimony.

- Others should comment first on that which was most helpful.
- Then suggestions for improvement should be offered.
- The group should try to draw out that which best expresses God's work in the person's life.
- Notes should be taken so that appropriate revisions can be made.

Once you receive their feedback, thank them for taking the time to help you. Revise your testimony after you've prayed through their comments. Remember, your goal is the be as effective as you can be at sharing the wonderful truth of what God has done in you!

The next chapter will show you many examples of testimonies that are being used right now to help others get into the Gospel with their friends, relatives, work associates, and neighbors.

Keep refining your testimony, and develop others to be the most effective witness you can be for Christ and His Kingdom!

Malcolm's Story
South Africa

I 've been involved with design of systems to secure buildings for many years and implemented many such systems in some fairly significant buildings. And, generally, they have sensors that monitor various conditions in the building to ensure that things are all kept within parameters and safe, so that if they would see smoke in an area, it would sound an alert. At the back end of that there is a control room with computers and screens with graphic layouts showing positioning of all the sensors that can actually direct you to where the problem is. And, essentially, if something like that happens, then the guys on duty would call up a response team and say, "Go investigate."

Having been involved with that for so many years, and also having been involved on the EE side, seeing amazing things in our time, I've realized that there is a strong parallel here. I see Heaven as a control room with the angels on duty, kind of parading on duty, watching the screens and as soon as somebody who is in trouble on earth cries out to God, it appears like a flashing light on the screen, and the angels immediately look at this and say, "Well, these are the coordinates, so let's have a look at where the nearest response teams are."

Now, how do they detect the response team? Well, the Bible says, *"Those who are wise shall shine like the brightness of the firmament, and those who turn many to righteousness like the stars forever and ever"* (Daniel 12:3 NKJV). So we are actually bright lights on this screen.

They may see four in a car moving from a Bible school or a church service, and say, "Fine, we just now need to move them two blocks east and one block south to make this connection." So they may cause a traffic jam or something else, so the guys in the car get frantic. They may feel they're late for something but then they see somebody that is in distress and suddenly their attention is there to minister.

I was driving back from Johannesburg and there was a hitchhiker on the side of the road. I had no intention of stopping because I was in a hurry to get back to my office. But as I passed him, I felt almost like a magnetic pull toward this guy and I swerved over to the side of the road. As I saw him come running to the car in my rear-view mirror, I had this feeling—I couldn't say it was a voice—but it was a message to me, saying, "Immediately, tell him the good news. Don't talk to him about anything else."

As soon as he got into the car, I said, "This is going to sound crazy to you, but I'd like to know, have you come to the place in your life where you know for sure that if you were to die today you would go to Heaven?"

That is very upfront.

And he looked at me and was stunned. He just said to me, "No."

But I could see this really had a very powerful impact on him.

He was a big strapping young man. A soldier dressed in uniform.

I said to him, "Well, do you know that it is possible to know without being a hypocrite?"

"No."

So I carried on and I shared the Gospel with him with his permission, and he was so emotional that I had to stop the car at the end. He wanted to accept the Lord. I prayed with him. When all of that was done, after he invited the Lord into his life, he said to me, "Malcolm, you need to know what's happened here. My life, up to this point, has been a total disaster. I took a decision this morning that there was no reason left for me to live. And I am AWOL from my military camp. I'm on my way to Johannesburg where my car's parked and I was going to go fetch my car and kill myself.

And as I was walking along the road, I said, "God, if there is a God, you'll reveal yourself to me. And shortly after that your car stopped."

Now, when I heard that, you can imagine, I was blown away. That did more for me than I think it did for him. I just realized, God is amazing. He loves this person so much that He would intervene and this young man would hear the good news.

That is the thing that has made me so passionate about this ministry and so passionate about getting others involved because I believe, every one of us, the minute we say, "Lord, here I am, I'm gonna share this with people, so please help me," then we become a dot on Heaven's radar screens. We become that connection point that God can use to connect us with people and it can change their lives.

There are many such incidents since then that have been astounding and every time they occur they lift me to a new level where I realize God is more aware and more around us than we know. And it's really that we are on assignment for Him.

SIX

WHATSMYSTORY.ORG
EXAMPLES OF TESTIMONIES PEOPLE ARE USING ON THE WEB

And they have defeated him [Satan] by the blood of the Lamb and by their testimony. And they did not love their lives so much that they were afraid to die.

Revelations 12:11 NLT

E vangelism Explosion International has developed a website called WhatsMyStory.org to assist you in developing and sharing your story. You will find many of the tools used in chapter five there online to help you to perfect your story. Once completed, you can attach a link to your story at the bottom of your emails, so that friends and family can read your story. At the bottom of your story there is a link to the Gospel, so that those who read your story can find out how it happened.

Our desire is to help facilitate the sharing of your story to the largest group of people possible. You're welcome to share that site with friends at church to help them begin this wonderful walk of sharing Christ with all that we can. Who knows how God will use your story in someone's life? And they may be in another state, country, or continent!

The following are examples of testimonies that you will find on the site. Perhaps they will help you in refining your own story. Regardless, I'm sure you'll rejoice with all of these brothers and sisters in Christ for the change that He has made in their lives.

CHILDHOOD CONVERSION TESTIMONY EXAMPLES

> TITLE: TRUE JOY AND COMFORT
> USER: ROGER
> DATE: OCTOBER 06, 2013

I'm glad I know that I have eternal life because of the comfort I have in knowing that I have a purpose for my life and an example to follow.

I would have friends in school try to get me to go to a party and drink. I was able to refuse and explain why. The next day in school I would ask if they had fun at the party and they would say yes, but couldn't remember what happened. Some of these friends have never done anything because of the drinking. I have been able to avoid it completely.

Jesus has made many promises in the Bible and has never broken one of them. By this, I have confidence that I will spend eternity with him in Heaven.

TITLE: DEALING WITH A DIFFICULT DIAGNOSIS
USER: DENTALGIRL
DATE: OCTOBER 27, 2013

I'm glad I know that I have eternal life because it creates an inner peace in my life when other areas are always crazy and out of my control.

When I was unexpectedly diagnosed with cancer and uncertain about what my future would be, I had a peace inside of me that I could not explain. Some of the fears I had did happen, but I was able to walk though that experience without those fears overcoming me. In fact, I would say that in going through that experience my life changed for the better in most aspects.

That same peace that God gave me during the treatment of my cancer is something that I experience every day of my life. I know without a doubt that God is always with me and that I will spend eternity with Him in Heaven.

> **TITLE: I'VE GOT THE JOY...DOWN IN MY HEART**
> **USER: RICHARD**
> **DATE: MARCH 25, 2009**

I now know that no matter what circumstance I find myself in, I can have true joy in it.

I remember during my sophomore year of college my mother was diagnosed with brain cancer. I was so worried about her and the operation, but I knew that no matter what happened I would see her one day again in Heaven.

That knowledge gave me peace during the whole thing.

ADULT CONVERSION TESTIMONY EXAMPLES

> **TITLE: FINDING LOVE IN HATE**
> **USER: LY K.**
> **DATE: SEPTEMBER 24, 2013**

Before I met Christ, I was afraid of people.

When I was younger, I was exposed to how people could lie, and how they may say one thing to your face, but say the opposite when you are not looking. I remember experiencing this and feeling like I could no longer trust anyone with anything that they said.

Then, I met Christ and He showed me how to love and trust others again.

Now, I can trust others, and I do not automatically assume that they are lying to me or that they hate me.

One summer as I was praying with my church, I felt a peace in my heart. And I knew that everyone in the room loved me, and that I was not being judged.

I used to think that the world was only filled with hate and judgment, but now I know that only God can judge me, and that the love of Jesus Christ is all that I need. And I know that if God were to take me right now, I would be in a place of eternal love and compassion with Him.

TITLE: FROM STORMY TO LOVING
USER: FRED P.
DATE: NOVEMBER 16, 2010

Before I received eternal life, my relationship with my parents was stormy and rebellious.

My step-father loved kids and had interesting hobbies (he would hunt, fish and ride motorcycles), but I wouldn't let him get close enough to be the father he wanted to be. I simply chose to go my own way.

Then someone shared with me how I could receive eternal life.

Now that I have eternal life, the relationship with my parents changed from stormy to pleasant.

As I learned how much God loved me in spite of myself, I began to love my parents also. I began to call my step-father "Dad," rather than by his first name. And eventually, I was able to tell him I truly loved him.

Better yet, the full life that Jesus offers lasts forever. If I were to die right now, I know for certain that I'd be with God in Heaven.

TITLE: MARCH 28, 1978
USER: CHERYL S.
DATE: OCTOBER 08, 2011

Before I received eternal life, my life lacked purpose.

While in college, I believed that I was my own source of morality; I could do as I pleased and if no one was hurt, what did it matter. My world revolved around ME. But I soon began wondering if there was more to life than selfishness. I envied the obvious peace and purpose a Christian friend seemed to have. One night I asked her what made the difference in her life. That is when she explained to me about Jesus.

112

I thought hard about what my friend told me. A few days later, I prayed, asking God to take control of my life.

Now that God is in my life, I have peace and purpose for my life.

For example, when we needed to move from the west coast to Ohio for my husband's work, God let me know that this was His will for us. Even though moving away from friends and family was hard, I had peace knowing He was with me and that this was His purpose for our lives.

Currently my aging parents still live out west. But they also are Christ followers. I have peace knowing that if either they or I died, we would someday be reunited with God in Heaven.

> TITLE: MY FEAR IS GONE!
> USER: JBSOREN
> DATE: SEPTEMBER 19, 2007

Before I received eternal life I was afraid of dying. My dad died when he was 42. It was pretty awful watching him die. He was terrified of dying and it really scared me. I wouldn't even go around someone that was dying because the thought frightened me so much.

Then, I received eternal life.

Right after that my fear of death went away. I was on a plane five days later. We took off from Chicago heading to Newark. The pilot came on and said, "Folks, we have a real problem. We don't have any hydraulic fluid. We use it to put the landing gear down. More than that, we use it to hold the landing gear down. I can still control the plane so we're going to go on to Newark and get rid of the fuel that we have. Then we're going to try to make a landing. If you know how to PRAY, NOW IS A GOOD TIME!" People began to panic all around me. That was the first moment that I knew I wasn't afraid to die.

The plane landed OK but the great part of that whole incident is that I know for sure that when I die I'm going to be with God in Heaven!

TITLE: SEEKING APPROVAL
USER: EMILY
DATE: OCTOBER 07, 2013

Before I received eternal life, I was afraid of not receiving approval from God or other people.

I always tried to earn good grades, attend church regularly, avoid drugs and alcohol, and be a morally upright person. Yet no matter how well I performed, I never felt completely accepted by anyone because I could never achieve perfection.

Then I received eternal life!

Now that I have eternal life, I have security in my relationship with God.

I don't have to be afraid of being rejected by God because I know I belong to Him for all eternity. And since I know He already accepts and loves me, I am free to obey Him out of gratitude and trust, instead of fear and uncertainty.

I have complete confidence that I will be with the Lord in Heaven when I die.

TITLE: IN PURSUIT OF REAL HAPPINESS
USER: KRISHNA S.
DATE: JUNE 12, 2012

Before I received eternal life I had wanted to die because my life had no meaning.

I remember standing at my brother's funeral a few years ago. All I could think about was where would I end up if I had died the way he chose to.

Then I was thankful that I have discovered true meaning to life years ago after someone shared with me how I could receive eternal life. At that moment, I began experiencing life as God wants for us.

Now that I have eternal life, I am satisfied and want to live life to its fullest.

One afternoon I was up on a coconut tree and I almost fell. Later that evening, before I went to bed, I reflected on this incident. I had peace knowing that if that were my time, I would go to Heaven.

Better yet, the life that I have found in Jesus lasts forever. If I were to die right now, I am certain that I would be with God in Heaven.

TITLE: DISCOVERING TRUE PEACE
USER: RICHARD W.
DATE: JANUARY 12, 2011

Before I received eternal life, I was afraid of dying.

As a child in the 1950s, I was terrified of the thought that the Cubans would launch a nuclear attack on us. Every time the early warning system was tested, I thought it was an attack. I was terrified. I had no idea what would happen to me if I was killed.

Then I discovered how to have eternal life.

Now that I have eternal life, I no longer have a fear of dying.

I found myself in the emergency room of a local hospital one Sunday evening. I had been suffering terrible pain for the past six months and had lost 40 pounds. X-rays were taken, and the doctor came in and told me I had a mass in my abdomen and that I should see a surgeon as soon as possible. He walked out, leaving me alone with my thoughts. It was then that I realized I had no fear of death or dying. I had peace in knowing that when I die, I will go to Heaven,

I can't imagine anything better than knowing that if I were to die in the next breath, I would go to be with God in His Heaven.

TITLE: FROM ANGER TO LAUGHTER
USER: MELODY Y.
DATE: OCTOBER 06, 2010

Before I received eternal life, I was an angry person. I was hostile towards people and God.

In college, I was referred to as the "Ice Queen". I had one emotion: anger. I didn't laugh and I hardly smiled. I told people I was going to hell and that I didn't care. I didn't want to talk about God to anyone.

Then some girls shared with me about eternal life and how God loved me.

Now that I have eternal life, I am no longer angry and hostile toward God or people.

I am now known for my laugh everywhere I go whether I am at church, work or in another public place. I can be in a crowded movie theatre and someone who knows me hears me laugh and they immediately know that I am present.

Because of the change in my outward countenance, I can never doubt that I belong to God. The change in my life has been so drastic that people who once knew me in college can hardly believe it. If I died today, I know for certain I'd be with God in Heaven.

> TITLE: IT'S NOT ABOUT ME, IT'S ABOUT HIM
> USER: JCOUNCE
> DATE: FEBRUARY 25, 2010

Before I received eternal life, I only lived for me and what I wanted, and this left me feeling very alone and empty.

I always needed someone around me whether it was a friend or a girlfriend. I didn't care about their needs. They were just filling a void. I knew that as soon as I got alone, I would have to face the emptiness I felt.

Then one day someone shared with me how I could receive eternal life.

From that day on, I never again felt empty or alone anymore.

Just two years ago, I was caught up in a struggle that was really only about my wants and desires, and it could have literally ended my marriage. But God was there with me the whole time, and he saw me (us) through it.

Better yet, He will always be with me and I know that one day I will spend eternity with Him in Heaven.

TITLE: I FOUND THE PURPOSE OF MY LIFE!
USER: JAMES C.
DATE: MARCH 13, 2010

I came from Taiwan. My religious background was a combination of Confucianism, Buddhism, Taoism and ancestor worship, like most of the people from Asia.

As a young man I liked to read those philosophy books, searching for the meaning and purpose of life. Finally, in a summer retreat camp for college students, I received the gift of eternal life.

After graduation from medical college, we had to do one year of military service. I was sent to Kinmen—a small island very close to Communist China. There was propaganda bombardment every other night, but I had no fear. Even once a cannon ball fell about 10 feet in front of me, but I had no fear because I knew where I would go when I died.

TITLE: ACHIEVING PEACE AND PURPOSE
USER: ANN S.
DATE: MARCH 10, 2010

Before I received eternal life, I had no hope or purpose to my life.

It really became apparent to me when I was in my early twenties. My mom, who was also my best friend, came down with ovarian cancer; and she died within a year. Afterward, I became severely depressed and lost a lot of weight. I got to a point that I even prayed to God to let me die; and in a way, I did.

I died to that old life when someone shared with me how I could have eternal life, and I grabbed on to it!

Now that I have eternal life, I have a hope, joy, and a peace inside me; and I have a purpose to my life.

Many things have happened to me since that time to show me just how much I have changed. In fact, a couple years ago I developed a heart arrhythmia and had to be hospitalized for it. Even though I still had three children at home, I did not lose that hope and peace I had inside me. There was an older lady there at the hospital beside me having significant health issues, and I was able to help and comfort her during my time there.

This peace and purpose to my life comes from knowing that I have eternal life and being sure that when I die, I will go to be with God in Heaven.

I encourage you to visit www.WhatsMyStory.org and write your own testimony there. You'll have the opportunity to link to your testimony in your emails to friends and family.

EE has also been developing an app for your cell phone that will allow you to keep a record of your Gospel conversations. It is called "eeHelps". It is available for both iPhone® and Android® devices. In this app, you can share your testimony link with anyone that you meet, just by entering their email address.

I hope you'll take advantage of these online tools to broaden the reach of your testimony and see what God will do through the story He has given you!

BRYAN'S STORY
SOUTH AFRICA

W hat I know of this story begins in 1983 in a small seaport town in South Africa. My brother came to visit me from his home in Vereeniging, South Africa. I was on a sailboat, which was my home at the time. My brother knew that I had decided to enter in a trans-Atlantic sailboat race to South America two years in the future, and he wanted to say goodbye before I sailed further south to prepare for the race.

He told me that when I got to the States, I should look up a guy named Jim Kennedy. My brother had just read his book and done a course of his. It was odd that he would talk about the United States as the States are not part of South America! But my brother is a nuclear physicist by degree, so I knew he was not having a problem with his geography. I did not think about that conversation with my brother again for years.

Two and a half years later, I was in a small seaport town in Uruguay, South America, living on a sailboat. I received a telex from the owner of the boat asking me if I could meet him in Miami in July.

We played around the South American coast, sailing to various ports just for the adventure. Five months later after sailing north through the Caribbean, I was sitting in a restaurant in St. Thomas USVI chatting to a fellow seafarer. I told him I was on the way to Miami. He suggested I sail on the Atlantic side of the Bahamas, enter through the Northwest Passage, and head for Fort Lauderdale. He said it was easy to find because there are two large red and white smokestacks visible from miles away. He also said that Fort Lauderdale was much better than Miami as a place to visit.

Who would ignore the advice of a fellow sailor? Within a week we set sail for Fort Lauderdale.

Our sail across the Florida Gulf was without incident, and at 4:30 a.m. I spotted what appeared to be the light on the smoke stacks that my acquaintance in St. Thomas had told me about. I asked the crew to stay on a heading toward the lights and to call me at sunrise. According to the nautical manual I had, the port opened at 7:30 a.m. When I came out on deck at sunrise, I realized we had been heading for a church steeple and not the smoke stacks. Because we were low on diesel and we were up current with no wind, we had to risk it and run the engines burning the last of the fuel to get to the entrance of Port Everglades.

Thankfully, we made it! Now my wife and I needed to figure out how to make a living in the States. We spent the next two years living on the sailboat while building a clothing business. Eventually we moved off the sailboat and into a shore side residence—my first in 10 years!

I walked into this first floor apartment and was totally impressed by how huge this two bedroom apartment was. I told our real estate agent that we would take it. But he argued with me. He said the homeowners association would drive me nuts because this was not a place for young people (My wife and I were 24 at the time). I argued back demanding that he rent to us. He relented, and we signed a lease.

We moved in shortly afterwards. All of our gear fit comfortably in our 1969 Chevy panel van. I had no sooner parked the vehicle in a spot in front of the apartment than the condo commander approached me and explained the by-laws of the apartment condos, which did not allow commercial vehicles. We shouted at each other for a while, I unpacked the van and drove off to look for parking elsewhere.

I returned to the apartment to inform Linda that I had found a suitable tree to park under next to a tennis court. I said it looked as though there was a big church there. Charlie, our real estate agent, had brought us to the apartment from the opposite direction, so we hadn't realized we were next to a church.

That Sunday, Linda suggested we visit the church.

The preacher that morning was none other than Jim Kennedy—the one my brother had told me about several years before. When Jim gave a sermon it was like a university lecture, and we loved it.

That day the sermon was on Noah's Ark. Jim had done his homework. He had the dimensions of the vessel, the cubic capacity, the draft, the size of the cargo to be loaded. It was a lecture of note, and I took notes…. This all made so much sense!

The next day Linda informed me that we were having a guest over that week. It was to be Jim Kennedy, and he wanted to welcome us to the community. This seemed like the American efficiency I had read about while in Africa, so I was looking forward to the visit.

Wednesday arrived. Jim Kennedy, his daughter Jennifer, and Dan Domin (an elder at the church) came for their visit. We offered them a glass of wine, which they declined, and spent about four hours socializing. Jim presented the Gospel of Jesus Christ to us—the Good News! He explained that Christ was calling us to accept his free gift of eternal life, and he asked if we would like to pray to receive it. Linda had been led to the Lord at a Billy Graham crusade in Africa; she was ready to pray. I suggested that it seemed like a sound concept and asked Jim if he could leave me a copy of the book to review. (I think I was referring to his Bible!)

Jim had gotten to know quite a bit about us prior to asking us to pray. He asked me to imagine that he and Linda were standing on the deck of our sailboat, and that I had fallen overboard in the water. He said he was ready to save me by throwing me the lifebuoy with a line attached, but that what I was effectively insisting on is that I first read the lifebuoy manual before trusting it.

Having recently practiced man-overboard procedures I knew how perilous a situation that would be with no time for hesitation. He suggested I hang on to the lifebuoy by praying with him to accept Jesus, and I could read the manual and ask as many questions as I needed later.

I prayed and accepted Jesus Christ into my life that night in February 1987.

Jesus Christ used Jim Kennedy and his church to influence our lives over the next 22 years. His teaching and that of his staff guided us and, I believe, saved our marriage.

Jim played tennis with me on several Monday mornings. Our children, Justin and Lauren, were christened, attended Sunday school, and were later educated preschool-12th grade at the church's school, Westminster Academy. Linda and I both taught children's Sunday school at the church, and we also went through evangelism training through the EE ministry.

Then we had a new neighbor move in next door to us because he and his family came down from Nebraska to work for EE. This was not surprising because we lived close to the church and ours was an ideal neighborhood for kids. Over the years, John (our new neighbor) would mention to Linda and me that we should be working in the ministry with him. I always agreed, and we would have a laugh and move on. This continued for about 12 years, with John making this comment a couple of times a year.

In 2007, our son Justin was diagnosed with cancer. Our lives took a different course.

We all prayed for Justin's health and comfort as he went through his treatment. We praised God for Justin's courage and incredible attitude throughout this ordeal. One Saturday, while Linda and I were doing our personal devotions, I said that I felt such gratitude to God and that I wondered if I could ever serve Him in some way. I prayed specifically about this.

I got up out of my chair and went out to my car to get something. While outside, John and his wife Ann walked up to me; and John said, "Bryan when are you going to be a part of the EE ministry? We need your help." I was a little rattled. I told him I was very involved in my current job. I offered to help them find someone. The next day, having thought about this most of the night, I contacted John and asked him if I could do some volunteer work to try and meet their need in the interim. John agreed to allow me to do this.

Over a period of months, I worked with John and his staff to prepare the annual budget for EE. I could not devote as much time as I would like because I was working 75 hours + a week trying to figure out how to do my day job well. The EE budget process went reasonably well, and we were able to come up with a few new ideas and produce a budget on time.

I waited to hear from John again. A few weeks later he called me from Australia at 2 a.m. (their time) and left me a message saying that EE really needed help in the area of business operations. When he returned from Australia, we met and discussed the possibilities. We had a conference call with a board member and they later offered me a position to be part of the ministry.

I was invited to attend the weekly EE devotional at 8:30 a.m. on Tuesday the week before I was to start my job at EE. This turned out to be my first day on the job because I was sucked into a workload immediately after devotions. I was introduced as the new chap, and the devotion was led by a man named Dr. Ron Kovack, a board member for EE.

When I had entered the conference room, there was a seat available at the end of the table next to Ron. I introduced myself and sat next to him. The room started to fill up, and I felt uncomfortable. I decided to move to one of the seats against the wall away from the table. I had read somewhere that it is better to be invited to the table than to be asked to leave it.

After the devotions, we had a list of 300 prayer requests from people that we needed to pray for. We broke into eight groups of four people each to pray for a section of the list. To decide who would be in which group, we went around the room, counting from one to eight. Whatever number you called out was the number of the group you were in. I happened to be in group one with Ron Kovack and John Sorensen, President of EE, a nice coincidence I thought.

As we walked across the office area to John's office, I bumped into Ron who was chatting to Rick Bond. Rick Bond said, "You have to love this guy [me] because he is from South Africa." Ron commented that that was great. He had been in South Africa in 1983 to a town called Vereeniging.

This is the first time I have heard the word Vereeniging pronounced by an American.

I said, "That is amazing! I was born in Vereeniging." Ron was surprised, and I relayed a little of the story of my brother. We went into John's office to pray. I do sometimes cry—not too often—but the tears were streaming down my cheeks. Ron prayed aloud for the people on his list, but he also prayed for me—about six times. He was obviously a little taken aback. When we got up to leave, Ron continued his South Africa story and told me that he was in South Africa, in 1983 with Dan Domin, teaching EE.

In 1983, my brother came to tell me about EE after learning of it in Vereeniging that year.

In 1987, Dan Domin was one of the EE team with Jim and Jennifer Kennedy who led Linda and I to the Lord in our apartment in Fort Lauderdale.

In 2008, Ron Kovack, who had visited Vereeniging with Dan Domin in 1983, led the devotion at my first ever devotion at EE. No one can remember when Ron had last led the devotions.

Had I not moved from my seat next to Ron in the conference room, I would have been in group number two, not with Ron and John in group number one.

To this day, no one else has approached to present the Good News of the Gospel to me! My life, my wife, my children and who knows what else was spared and transformed by God and the Holy Spirit leading others to share the Good News with us.

How can we resist being a witness as well?

SEVEN

SHARE YOUR AMAZING STORY

LOOK AND BE AMAZED AT WHAT GOD HAS DONE

And Moses said to the people, "Do not be afraid. Stand still, and see the salvation of the Lord, which He will accomplish for you today."

Exodus 14:13 NLT

God's plan is truly marvelous. One of the most amazing things about being on this journey with Him is that we get to see how His Providential Hand guides and leads us. The so-called "miracles" or "coincidences" are really God working in and through our lives in order to create a masterpiece of His plan for this world. It is like a big, beautiful tapestry being woven together.

Every strand is important in order to show the beauty of the picture that the grand tapestry makes; however, if you are miss-

133

ing even one thread, the picture would be marred and incomplete.

Our stories are like those strands—pieces in God's story for this world to see. When combined together, we begin to get a view of what God is doing in and through His people. We may not be able to see the big picture here on earth, but someday when we are sitting in glory in the presence of Christ our Savior and Lord, we will be able to see the picture put together of what God has done; and is doing in the lives of Christians still on earth. I know that we will marvel at it for all eternity.

In Bryan's story, you can see how God planned and orchestrated every detail. What are the chances that Ron Kovack and Dan Domin would hear the call of God and go to South Africa in 1983? What are the chances that Bryan's brother would be there to hear them? How could it be that Bryan would head for what he thought was a smokestack, but turned out to be the steeple of a church? Later, he would park at that church where the pastor was none other than the one that his brother had told him about! How could Dan Domin be on the team that came to share the Gospel with him and help lead him to a decision to accept Christ? What are the chances that Ron Kovack would end up teaching devotions on Bryan's first day of working in ministry? No one but God could put all of that together!

I am thoroughly convinced that there is no such thing as coincidence in this world. God is sovereign and works all things together in order to be glorified through the process. Without Him, how could this happen? How could every detail be put in place in such a way?

God works the same way in your life too. We all have stories of "coincidences" or "miracles" where no one but God could have been moving and working in our lives. They are stories that when we live through them, the people who are around us who get to see what God is doing say, "Your God can do anything!"

When Ann and I were called into the EE ministry in November of 1996, God worked a series of miracles in our lives that firmly planted us in full-time ministry. I was amazed at all that God did to make our coming to Fort Lauderdale happen. And I am so glad that I had the presence of mind to write them down.

We saw God do seven miracles that simply couldn't be done apart from Him.

First, He changed Ann's heart. Right after we came to know Jesus as our Savior and Lord, we believed that God had called us into ministry. We just didn't know when or where. We imagined that it would be once we retired. Perhaps we could be dorm parents at a missionary school. But in the fall of 1996, God told me where and when.

I remember the day that I told Ann that I felt it was time to go. We had just purchased a farm house out in the middle of the country. Ann loved it. We had begun to fix it up. After only six months, it was a beautiful house with fields and barns. So, on the day that I told Ann what I felt God had said, her first reply was, "No! Absolutely not. I will not go! We just got here!"

But she began to pray, and God revealed to her as well that it was time to go. One week later, she told me that she had heard from God, too.

But this was winter. Our farm house was on a dirt road. Every bit of counsel that we received told us that it was impossible to sell a farm house in January. No one could even remember a house in Shelby County, Iowa, ever selling in January—not once! The second miracle was that He sold our house on the first day it was on the market.

Next, they told us that we could never get the price we needed out of the house. We had fixed it up so that it was the most expensive house in the county. No house had ever sold for what we were asking there! The third miracle was that God gave us every penny of what we asked.

Fourth, they said we could never get it to appraise for the value that we were asking, as there were no comparable sales in the county where we lived. I remember the day when the appraiser came out. We made the best case we could and showed him before and after pictures of all that we had done. He went out to his car and remained there quite a long while. Finally, he came back up and showed us the appraisal. It was all that we would need.

Next, we were told that the buyers would never be able to get a loan as the bank would not want to finance the most expensive house in the county. They made us jump through some hoops but guess what? The fifth miracle came when God moved the bank to give the buyers the loan. Our real estate agent, who was not a believer, said, "Your God can do anything!" Yes, He can.

Now, we were on our way to Fort Lauderdale! God showed us a wonderful house in Florida that we really felt was the right place for us there. But the truth was, we couldn't afford it.

I had already told the company that I worked for that we would be leaving the first week of April. After I told them, I found out that the company was going to cut about ten jobs from the Central Region team.

One day, while at the office in Chicago, my Central Region Director asked me to come into his office. He told me that he had heard that I was leaving. And that he knew my wife had some medical issues that would make it difficult for us if we were without insurance for a period of time (often companies do not put you on their plan until you have been with them for at least three months). He reached behind him onto his credenza and grabbed a package, then handed it to me. He said, "I know I don't have to do this. But I'm going to. Here is a severance package. It provides six months of insurance, the vesting of your savings, and some money to help you get started in Florida."

We needed right at $15,000 more than what we had to buy the house. Want to take a guess at how much the severance money was? $15,100! God had provided $100 for a dinner out to celebrate! And that was miracle six.

Miracle seven was how He provided our support. All of the staff at EE raise their support (with the exception of some of the support staff). We really didn't know how to do that. We had come close, but were still about $7,000 off. So, we were praying. I remember my boss saying, "You really have to get that raised in the next two weeks or we will have to reduce your pay." Whew!

That Friday I received a call from the administrator of the Missions Committee at Coral Ridge Presbyterian Church. She asked, "Why haven't you applied for missionary funds from the church?" I had never heard of such a thing. She said, "We have a meeting Sunday, and am saving some money for you, but you have to apply for it today." I think I was in her office before we hung up the phone! We filled out the papers and Sunday night we had $4,000 of the $7,000 in hand.

Monday, just one week after being told we need to raise the $7,000, I was out of the office, speaking at a conference. When I came back in that evening there was an envelope on my desk. In it was a check and a note. The note said, "We really felt God tell use to give you this." It was a check for $3,000 from a couple that we had just met at church.

By the time God was done with His seven miracles, we couldn't help but trust Him.

In Revelation 12:11, we are told that we will overcome Satan, *"By the blood of the Lamb and by their testimony."* That is the power of the story of God in us. And it's spoken of in the same sentence as the precious blood of our Savior, Jesus Christ.

Ultimately, we know that our story is really God's story, but He tells it daily in and through our lives. In the process, He builds our faith and shows others the truth about His wonderful grace and faithfulness.

Life is one big opportunity to look for and discover these amazing stories. Never call them plain, simple, or unimportant.

My challenge to you is that you find at least one of your stories. Refine it and learn it well. Then begin to look for opportunities to share it. And as you do, you will bring glory and honor to God's great name.

EVANGELISMEXPLOSION.ORG

WHATSMYSTORY.ORG

PERSONAL TESTIMONY WORKSHEET

(For use if converted as an adult)

I. Before I received eternal life ...

    A. State one life concept (i.e., worry, fear of death, lack of purpose).

    B. Illustrate this concept with specific examples(s) from your own life (use pictorial or descriptive language).

II. Then I received eternal life.

III. Now that I have eternal life ...

    A. State the reverse of concept I-A above (how God completed your life with peace, freedom from fear, or purpose).

    B. Give reverse illustration of I-B above from your own life (use descriptive language).

    C. Always include the statement that you know you have eternal life and that you are going to Heaven when you die.

    D. Transition: "May I ask you a question?"

Personal Testimony Worksheet

(For use if converted in childhood)

I. I'm glad I know that I have eternal life because ...

A. State one positive life concept (i.e., peace, security, purpose).

B. Illustrate this concept with a specific example from your own life (use pictorial or descriptive language).

C. Always include a statement that you know that you have eternal life and that you are going to Heaven when you die.

D. Transition: "May I ask you a question?"

143

MAKE THE CONNECTION
by DR. JAMES F. ENGLE

"This volume is dedicated to seeking out, amplifying and applying the connections that the Lord makes as He holds and works all things together for our good and His glory. Each chapter highlights one of these connections. To coin a phrase, I am calling them 'doctrinal devotionals.' You may find some of these connections logical and obvious. I have included them because, although logical and obvious, they are often ignored. They deal with the very basics of living with Christ as Lord. Other connections only become apparent as one's biblical knowledge and understanding deepen. These need to take root in our lives as spiritual growth takes place. Daily, regular and disciplined time invested into the Word of God brings about that continued work of the Spirit in conforming us to the image of Christ. Still other connections, on the surface, appear to be contradictions. They are not. They are clear expressions of the radical nature of the Gospel and its implication for our lives. These challenge the areas where our fallen nature and our increasingly godless culture seek to press us into its mold. Abraham Kuyper wrote, 'In the total expanse of human life there is not a single square inch over which Christ, who alone is sovereign, does not declare, That is Mine!' We all have territory in our lives that we are attempting to own and control. It is my prayer that the Lord will use these doctrinal devotionals to lead us to relinquish those territories to the control of our Lord. After all, the territory really is already His."

BUY IT AT:

EVANGELISM EXPLOSION
I N T E R N A T I O N A L
https://evangelismexplosion.org/store/

Green Tree Press

Green Tree Press

MORE BOOKS FROM GREENTREE PRESS:

GREEN by
ARCHBISHOP HARRY GOODHEW

Modern Christianity in the West tends to be plagued with a great deal of shallowness. We are a mile wide and an inch deep. *Green* digs into the issues of growing deeply in Christ and sinking your roots into the promises, encouragements, and convictions found in Scripture. This book's purpose is to help you reconnect with some of the great spiritual disciplines found in God's Word that are the basis and foundation of spiritual growth.

Are you unsatisfied with keeping God and your spiritual walk on rocky, shallow grounds? Or are you close with God but looking for a reminder or refresher on keeping your relationship growing? Regardless of where you are in your Christian walk, the key growth factors found in *Green* are sure to be helpful in blossoming your relationship with our Savior, Jesus Christ, and living ever more in love with Him. May we all grow into the fullness of Christ until the day we arrive as a fruitful tree in the presence of Love Himself.

BUY IT AT:

EVANGELISM EXPLOSION
I N T E R N A T I O N A L
https://evangelismexplosion.org/store/

Green Tree Press